Early praise for this new edition of
Cross-Cultural Communication: A Visual Approach

"Richard has done it again. This is a very pleasant way to understand better the need for cross-cultural communication in increasingly global business. To be humble and show respect are only some of the qualities required to understand the benefits of cross-cultural communication. This book should be mandatory for everyone, not only people in the cross-cultural business."

Jorma Halonen, Executive Vice President & Deputy CEO, Volvo Group

"Richard Lewis' penetrating and insightful diagrams illustrating the communication styles of over 70 cultures are excellent examples of how a visual approach can enhance veracity. This book is a 'must' for trainers in the intercultural field."

Reinhard F. Leiter, Senior Vice President, Head of Executive Events, Allianz SE

"Richard Lewis' latest book on cross-cultural communication must be a one-off in its genre. It is particularly meaningful and useful for Japanese, Chinese, Korean and Vietnamese people, inasmuch as the 'Visual Approach' is perfect for quick understanding for those cultures whose own writing is pictographic. As the saying goes: 'One picture is worth 1,000 words'. Japanese and other Asian universities will find this book an invaluable tool in acquiring insight into the mental processes behind the communication styles of the world's cultures."

Kuni Kawamura, former Head of Daiwa Securities Europe

"We live in a global milieu where acts of speech between nations are increasingly structured by the protocols of command. In this context, where language assumes the nature of imperative – the imposition of a dominant will upon a subordinate one – Richard Lewis' *Cross-Cultural Communication: A Visual Approach* is a timely reminder about the ethics of 'communication'. The process of learning to speak to others and, concomitantly, learning to listen, not only assists in the creation of decent human sociality, it is also a more efficient way of persuading and influencing interlocutors, audiences, colleagues. This thoughtful, insightful and pragmatic text is a valuable guide for all those committed to the democratisation of speech in the public and professional sphere."

Leela Gandhi, Professor of English Literature and Language, The University of Chicago

Other books by Richard D. Lewis

When Cultures Collide (1996, 1999, 2006)
Nicholas Brealey Publishing, London, UK

Humour across Frontiers: Round the World in 80 Jokes (2005)
Transcreen Publications, Winchester, UK

Finland, Cultural Lone Wolf (2005)
Intercultural Press, Yarmouth ME, USA

The Cultural Imperative: Global Trends in the 21st Century (2003)
Intercultural Press, Yarmouth ME, USA

Memoirs of a Linguist: The Road from Wigan Pier (1998)
Transcreen Publications, Winchester, UK

The Billingers (1976)
Riversdown Publications, London, UK

Cambridge 2000 (1971)
Linguasonica, Lisbon, Portugal

Travelling Abroad (1971)
Libraria Francisco Franco, Lisbon, Portugal

Reading for Adults (1968)
Longman, London, UK

Vous-souvenez-vous (1959)
Publitur, Lisbon, Portugal

Suomen Kirja (1958)
Berlitz, Helsinki, Finland

English You Need (1958)
Publitur, Lisbon, Portugal

Cross-Cultural Communication

A Visual Approach

*A Major New Edition
of the
Visual Guide to Cross-Culture*

by

Richard D. Lewis

Transcreen
– Publications –

Cross-Cultural Communication: A Visual Approach

First published in 1999 by Transcreen Publications.
This revised edition first published in 2008.

Transcreen Publications
The Old Stables
Warnford
Hampshire
SO32 3LH
United Kingdom

Tel. +44 (0)1962 77 11 11
Fax +44 (0)1962 77 10 50
Email info@transcreen.net

ISBN: 978-0-9534398-3-6

Layout and cover design by David Lewis Art (www.davidlewisart.com).
Cartoons by Kaj Wallen.
Printed in Finland by WS Bookwell.

To my cousin Adrian

How to find your way around this book

The book is divided into five chapters and an appendix as follows:

Communication Patterns at Meetings
Listening Habits
Audience Expectations during Presentations
Leadership Styles
Language of Management
Appendix

Each chapter (excluding the appendix) comprises the following sections:

The British Isles
Western Europe
Nordic & Baltic States
Central & Eastern Europe
Middle East
Central Asia
Asia
Africa
Australasia
North America
South America & Caribbean

Use the indexes & contents page opposite to locate specific combinations of culture and function.

For example, to find a description of the French leadership style, go to page xii, locate "France" in the "Western Europe" section, and look across for the page number.

Alternatively, you can use the Alphabetical Index on pages xiv-xv to locate any culture and function combination quickly.

Indexes & Contents

Indexes

Contents

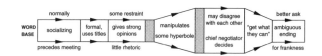

Communication Patterns at Meetings

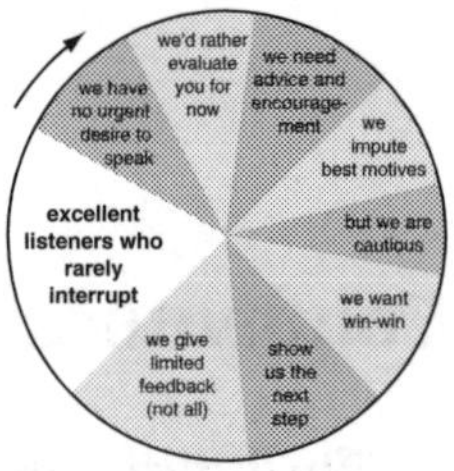

Listening Habits

Audience Expectations during Presentations

Leadership Styles

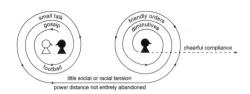

small talk
gossip
football
little social or racial tension
power distance not entirely abandoned

friendly orders
diminutives
cheerful compliance

Language of Management

Alphabetical Index

	Communication Patterns	Listening Habits	Audience Expectations	Leadership Styles	Language of Management
Jamaica	54	112	131	188	246
Japan	36	94	127	170	228
Korea, South	38	96	127	172	230
Korea, North	38	96	127	172	230
Latvia	18	76	122	152	210
Lithuania	18	76	122	152	210
Malaysia	42	100	128	176	234
Mexico	50	108	130	184	242
Myanmar	40	98	128	174	232
Netherlands	8	66	119	142	200
New Zealand	48	106	130	182	240
Norway	16	74	121	150	208
Pakistan	34	92	125	168	226
Philippines	38	96	127	172	230
Poland	20	78	122	154	212
Portugal	10	68	120	144	202
Romania	22	80	123	156	214
Russia	26	84	124	160	218
Scotland	2	60	118	136	194
Serbia & Montenegro	24	82	123	158	216
Singapore	42	100	128	176	234
Slovakia	22	80	123	156	214
Slovenia	24	82	123	158	216
South Africa, black	46	104	129	180	238
South Africa, white British	46	104	129	180	238
South Africa, white Dutch	46	104	129	180	238
Spain	8	66	119	142	200
Sweden	14	72	121	148	206
Switzerland	8	66	119	142	200
Thailand	40	98	128	174	232
Turkey	28	86	124	162	220
Ukraine	26	84	124	160	218
United Kingdom (see England, Scotland, or Wales)					
USA	50	108	130	184	242
Vietnam	40	98	128	174	232
Wales	4	62	118	138	196

Appendix

Preface

Subsequent to the success and widespread distribution of the first edition of "Cross-Cultural Communication: A Visual Approach" (1999), I have in this edition increased the number of diagrams and descriptive texts from 118 to over 360, bringing in illustrations relative to approximately 45 countries that did not feature in the first edition.

In addition, some of the old diagrams have been improved on account of cultural or political changes and descriptive texts have been lengthened in many cases.

An important addition to the book is the appendix entitled "Affective Communication". This section lists various communication gambits which could be described as **affective** or **manipulative**. Although this type of communication seeks to influence the recipient by applying its own strategies and for its own purposes, we need not consider it as particularly negative. It is, in fact, generally well-meaning, as it is often used to avoid upsetting or embarrassing one's interlocutor. Finally I have included advice to the reader in the form of some **Golden Rules** as to how one should best communicate with the different cultural categories.

Richard D. Lewis
1st January 2008

Riversdown House
Warnford
Hampshire
SO32 3LH
United Kingdom

Introduction

Communication – verbal communication, that is – appears on the surface to be a relatively simple operation requiring two basic components – a speaker and a listener.

But we know it is a more complex process than that. Even when two people with a similar cultural background are involved, there are several stages between delivery and comprehension. First, words are spoken, but the actual message emerges only when the words are considered in context. What is said must be evaluated against the background of how it was said, when and where, who said it and why. There is also the filter created by the speaker's personality and psychological make-up.

The listening process, too, is complicated. Firstly the listener had certain expectations which were or were not met. The filter of the listener's personality colours the speech he/she hears. An interpretation is placed on the words, thus defining the message for the recipient. The intended message and the received one are rarely the same.

When the speaker and listener are from different cultures, the odds against an accurate interpretation of the message are great. Diverse backgrounds of history, customs, traditions and taboos, as well as the accepted manners of communicating in different parts of the world, interfere with straight comprehension. Speech is often intended to influence or manipulate our fellow man. Leadership and some form of dominance are often involved. Finally each language of the world has certain in-built characteristics, often unperceived by the people who speak them.

In each culture the patterns of communication, listening and manipulation are remarkably consistent. Once these are recognized by an outsider, the behaviour of the cultural group becomes more predictable. This book purports to give the international traveller a quick reference guide, in diagrammatic form, as to how different nationals expect to communicate with and influence interlocutors, audiences, colleagues and business partners.

Communication Patterns at Meetings

Meetings give individuals a chance to communicate – to use their speech skills to good effect. Speech is certainly a personal weapon, but different cultures use it in diverse ways.

Perhaps the most basic use of speech is to give and receive information. Germans, Finns, Dutch people are good at conveying facts, figures, etc., quickly and efficiently. Other cultures believe speech can be a much more powerful weapon in terms of eloquence, fluency and persuasion. Italians, particularly, believe they can convince anyone of just about anything, provided they gain sufficient personal access. French, Spaniards, South Americans use speech to great effect and at length, though Nordics and some Anglo-Saxons find it all too much at times.

Indians are very fond of flowery Victorian-like speech to inspire people. Russians like to search their souls verbally. Confucian and South-East Asian cultures use speech as a give-and-receive-respect mechanism and establish relative status and rank in a few sentences. Americans often launch into speech with business or selling in mind. Arabs use it in a didactic or moralistic manner.

In some less democratic societies, speech may be used for coercion, propaganda or deception. In some cultures, speech can be deployed in such a vague way that it actually clouds issues rather than clarifies them. English and Japanese people can waffle and stall with ease, while Chinese and Polynesians excel in ambiguity.

Silence itself is a form of speech when applied at appropriate moments and should not be interrupted! Finns and Japanese are past-masters at soothing or strategic silences.

Australians regard suitably broad speech as a mechanism for a manager to show solidarity with "the mates".

Finally some nationalities seem to love speech for the sake of speech itself, taking the stage to hear their own voice. French, Spanish and Greek people often perorate in this manner. They are not popular with Nordics and most Asians.

England

In England a meeting will probably be concluded successfully if one doesn't "rock the boat". Humour, understatement, vagueness, stalling, re-packaging and a sprinkling of white lies are all weapons for keeping it all jolly nice, chaps.

Scotland

Conversations and business discussions in Scotland are characterised by warm, folksy opening remarks, often flavoured with dry humour. Soon after, however, Scots like to get to the point quickly and their initial proposals are very direct and ring honest. When resisted, they are willing debaters, and, though tenacious, are not averse to making concessions if they get something in return. When under-resourced, or operating from a weaker position, they will salvage what they can from a less than perfect deal, as long as their reputation is left intact.

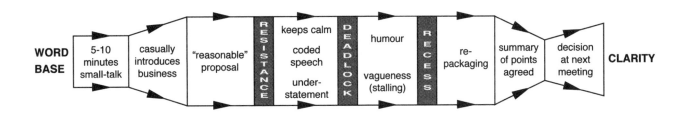

'don't rock the boat'

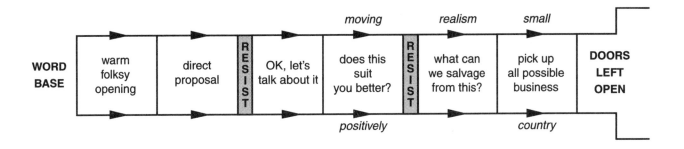

Ireland

Irish people speak in a more animated manner than the English and have been described as "audacious in speech". This audacity often borders on hyperbole and not infrequent embroidery of the truth. This results in what the Irish call "blarney" and must be taken into account when conversing with them. Warmly informal at all times, the Irish are great improvisers during discussions and resemble the Italians in their skill at showing apparent agreement and compliance. They are definitely more poetic and philosophical in speech than the English and have an unusual turn of phrase.

Wales

Welsh people are generally more friendly than (southern) English people in business meetings, often to the extent of being downright folksy. It is a "small country" attitude, which prizes direct and simplified discussion as the best and quickest route to doing business. When resisted they are capable of appearing naïve, even rustic – this being a disarming tactic which equates with English coded speech (to avoid upsetting people). Welsh frequent humour serves to hide their (mild) tenacity. They can be good losers in business, but want to win as much as anybody else. They are shrewder than they appear.

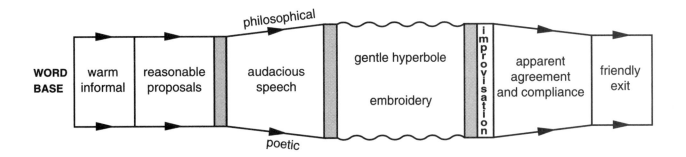

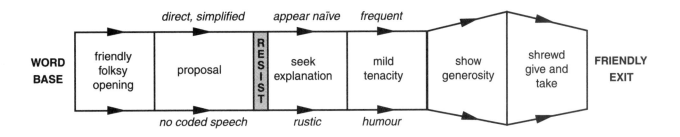

Germany

The German communication style is frank, open and direct. Truth comes before diplomacy. Many foreigners are surprised by the directness and honesty of Germans. Arguments are well-thought out, logical and weighty. Their speech style is serious, often unsmiling and frequently repetitive. Germans do not seek humour in a work context, even when a joke may lighten the atmosphere. They do not look for a light working climate. There are few taboo subjects in Germany, and for many Germans, none at all.

Italy

Italians are great communicators and lose all sense of time when engaged in interesting or intimate conversation. The style is intense, theatrical, emotional. Discussions may seem inordinately lengthy, unduly verbose, exceedingly penetrating and personal. When making proposals, they often launch into an initial version of 5,000 words or more. If they are then required to clarify or are disagreed with, they become more explicit and may give half an hour's clarification of the original proposal. In Italy words cost nothing.

France

Communication style is extrovert, personal, often emotional, but adheres to logic. The French are very explicit at most times. Managers give clear orders and staff react quickly. They hate vagueness and have trouble with the British in this respect. Though wanting clear instruction, French staff dislike being told anything twice. They always assume that the person they are talking to is intelligent. French "orators" are perhaps the best in the world.

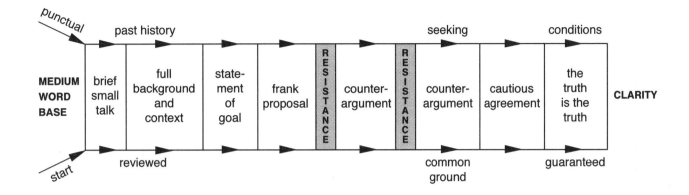

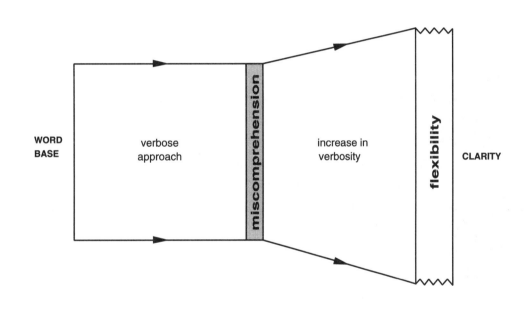

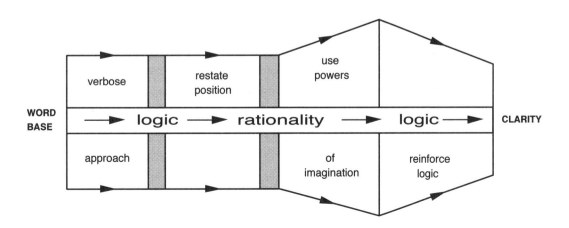

Switzerland

The Swiss are extremely polite conversationalists, in both social and business situations. Their desire for privacy and propriety leads them to carry on discourse in a pragmatic and detached manner. They shun inquisitiveness and rarely pry. They are not exciting speakers; even the French Swiss lack the charisma and rhetoric of their cousins in France. Swiss Italians (in the Ticino) are more open but, living in a prosperous area, they display a smugness less noticeable among Italians over the border.

Spain

Spanish proposals at meetings are usually delivered in a theatrical, declamatory fashion, which means that if they are delivered by a VIP, they are virtually irreversible. In such situations it is better to agree with everything, as Spanish luminaries cannot stand being opposed in public. Speakers begin to like and develop a loyalty towards compliant foreigners, to whom they are well disposed to make concessions over dinner later.

The Netherlands

The pragmatic Dutch, though mainly concerned with facts and figures, are also great talkers and rarely make final decisions without a long "Dutch debate", sometimes running the danger of over-analysis. Foreign counterparts are also subjected to this and routinely tested for bluffing, as Dutch people, with their long international experience in business, hate to think of themselves as being in any way gullible. They are not excitable and remain calm during discussion. They promise only that which they can deliver. They show little friendliness in the early stages of contact, but become warmer once a relationship has been established.

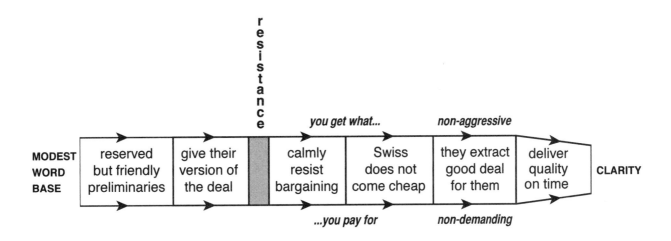

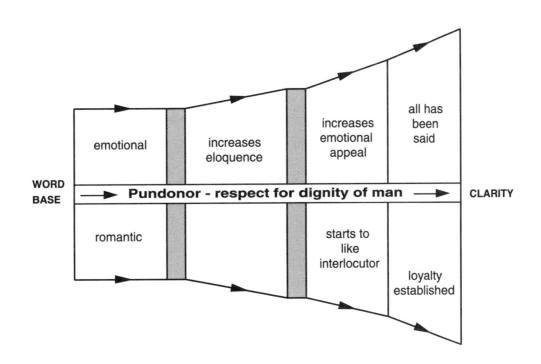

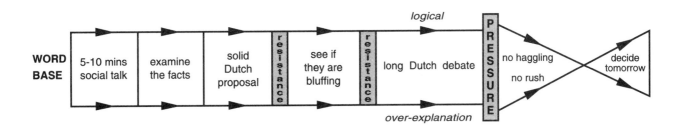

Austria (Vienna)

Austrians are efficient communicators, using charm and small talk, and on the surface are open and friendly. They are also manipulative, but in an unconscious, natural way, not cold and calculating. They are eager talkers in monologue and are raconteurs who love telling stories and embellishing as they go along. In business discussion their weakness is that they often lapse into a rambling, convoluted style, feeling that they have to fill in all the background and context. Nordic or American directness is disconcerting to Viennese, who find it "uncivilised".

Austria (Tirol)

In the Tirol, the speech style is more Germanic and straightforward. Less loud than Germans, they are open to occasional shafts of humour, but are mainly serious debaters.

Portugal

Portuguese are loquacious, eloquent and logical. Their roundabout style may confuse northern Europeans and Americans, but their final propositions are generally made clear. They like confirmation of agreements in writing. Telephone conversations tend to be protracted and verbose. They do their utmost to win the friendship and confidence of their interlocutor.

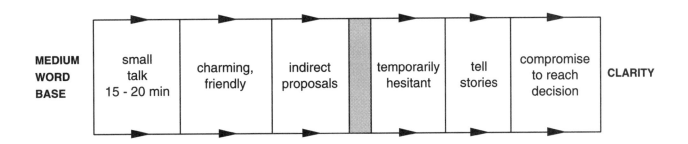

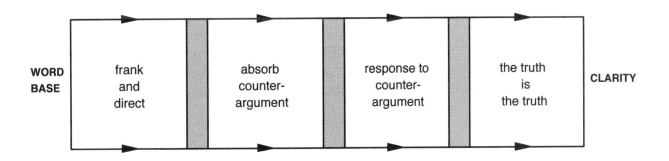

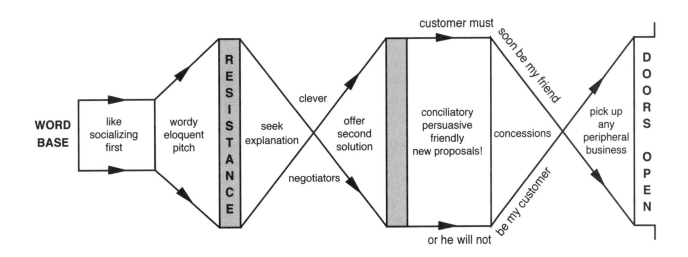

Belgium (Flemish)

Communication is informal as the boss mixes with staff and often acts on their ideas as well as his/her own. Facts are seen as more important than theories. As in Sweden, some form of consensus is mandatory. Solutions are gradualist rather than immediate.

Belgium (Walloon)

Communication goes through official channels, as there is a definite hierarchy in place. Walloons are more imaginative than Flemings, but avoid French rhetoric in favour of a toned-down Gallic style. Leaders and senior managers are more highly visible than is the case with Flemings and generally dominate discussion.

Greece

Greeks are verbose, theatrical and intense. Language is declaimed in a manner similar to Spanish; eye contact during address is strong. Emotion is used as a weapon in discourse. Greeks believe in their own powers of oratory. They use rational argument like the French, but spice it up with emotive content.

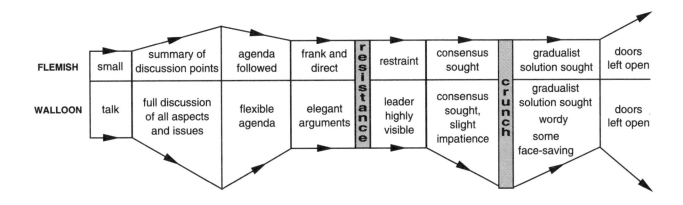

FLEMISH	small	summary of discussion points	agenda followed	frank and direct	resistance	restraint	consensus sought	gradualist solution sought	doors left open
WALLOON	talk	full discussion of all aspects and issues	flexible agenda	elegant arguments	resistance	leader highly visible	consensus sought, slight impatience	gradualist solution sought wordy some face-saving	doors left open

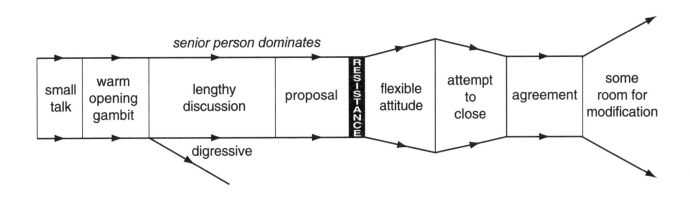

senior person dominates

small talk	warm opening gambit	lengthy discussion	proposal	RESISTANCE	flexible attitude	attempt to close	agreement	some room for modification

digressive

Finland

At meetings, Finns believe in saying only that which is absolutely necessary. Like the Japanese, they do not really trust words. If their original proposal is considered unclear, they repeat it in summarised form, assuming that is the best route to clarity. ("What I really meant was A, B and C"). An Italian counterpart sits waiting for the rest of the alphabet! Finns display Asiatic rather than European communication patterns. Being reactive by nature, Finns encourage others to speak first and respond carefully and usually after a pause. Finns value silence and will often use this when communicating as a sign of respect, without negative meaning. Statements are regarded as promises and are therefore delayed until the speaker is sure of his/her intentions. Finnish communication is typically frank and direct; exaggerated or emotive content and rhetoric are not welcomed or are seen as inappropriate and even comical.

Sweden

Swedes are quiet, reasonable negotiators, rarely using pressure or aggressive tactics. Compromise is seen as a solution to most disputes. Swedes are fond of attending meetings which they set up with the proper protocol. Amongst themselves they go on endlessly, but, when running up against foreign resistance, they ask for adjournment, so they can form a proper Swedish consensus. This tactic leads to considerable delays and frustrates go-getters like Americans, who wish to see early action. Swedish fondness for doing things the Swedish way often poses problems.

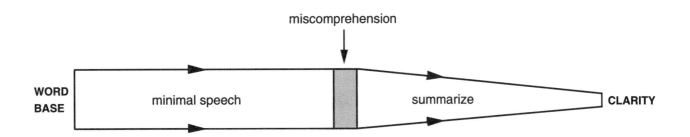

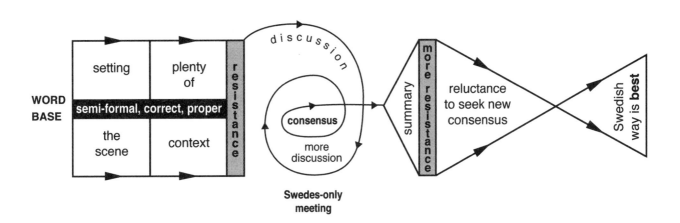

Denmark

Danes are fluent speakers but calm and low-voiced. They are the most loquacious of the five Nordic countries, though not obtrusively so. Swedes, Finns and Norwegians consider them somewhat facile and clever. Serious discussions are frequently interspersed with humour. They have a sense of humour which is close to Anglo-Saxon. Their linguistic ability is outstanding, particularly in English and German. Danes believe they can carry everybody (especially foreigners) by charm (in Danish "hygge") and seem to agree to all proposals well into the negotiation. They are skilful at subtle re-packaging and therefore have to be watched carefully. They are not happy at being "roped in", but maintain equanimity with an eye to future business.

Norway

Norwegians' sterling qualities and warm feelings are not readily communicated in their speech style. Cold climates tend to produce introverts and the Norwegians, along with the Finns, are the shyest of Europeans. Correspondence courses are big business in Norway on account of the sheer length of the country and the mountainous terrain, rendering physical accessibility a problem. Registration for English language courses is naturally very high, but by far the greatest number of enrolments, year in and year out, are for Public Speaking. Norwegians distrusted their ability to speak in public, but were secretly ambitious to learn how to do so, especially if they could take the course by correspondence! Norwegians, who rarely speak at too great a length, make their points well and use logic to back them up. They have a "fresh air" speaking style and like to convey a healthy, vigorous attitude. They can be quite ironic and indulge in their own brand of humour whenever the occasion arises.

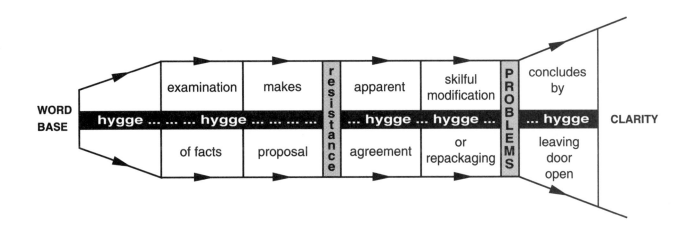

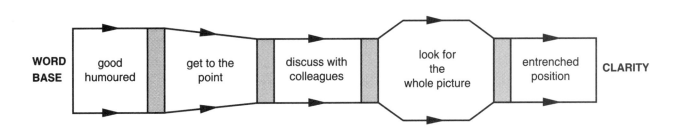

Estonia

Estonian speech style is slow and drawn-out. They do not rush to express an opinion. They see themselves as reserved, critical, closed, stubborn and wooden. Their body language gives very few clues away – no gestures, no noticeable movement and the face also may not register any emotions. Self-praise is not considered polite – modesty is a virtue. This sometimes causes problems in that people undervalue themselves. Business people have to be good at making speeches that are appropriate to the situation and the audience. Long speeches are considered boring.

Latvia

Latvians prefer a serious approach, in which open displays of emotionality or lightheartedness may be a barrier to the establishment of trust. However they do have a sense of humour. Slow, considered speech is best accepted in Latvia. Latvians are sometimes reluctant to volunteer information or to reveal thoughts. They are individualists in the sense that they are reserved among people strange to them. When they know someone well (including foreigners), they become much more communicative and sociable. Their style is typically formal and well-presented.

Lithuania

The Lithuanians are less reserved than Latvians and Estonians and are regarded by the former as talkative, even loquacious. Poles, however, consider them cold. Level of education is quite high and conversations are interesting, at times riveting. Their opinions are often laced with romantic idealism and nostalgia. They are certainly more communicative than their Northern neighbours.

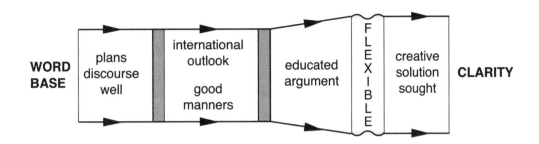

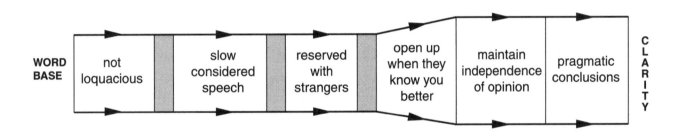

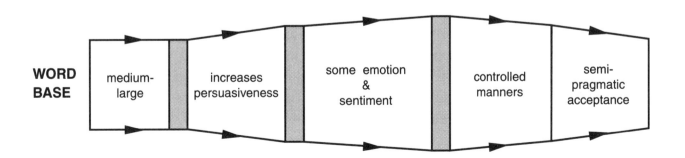

Poland

The Polish communication style is enigmatic. They can ring all the changes between a matter-of-fact pragmatic style and a wordy, sentimental, romantic approach to a given subject. When in the latter mode, they are fond of metaphor and their speech is rich in implied meaning, allusions, images and ambiguity. Irony and even satire are used to great effect. Thoughts are often expressed in a roundabout manner, assuming the listener will deduce what the real meaning is. One has to listen carefully for nuances and "read between the lines". Polish politeness and respect precludes too much directness, although they are occasionally quite sharp in their comments, particularly when discussing politics.

Hungary

Discussions with Hungarians can be deceptive in the extreme. They possess ample reserves of charm and charisma and give the impression that they are easy-going. They truly regard conversation as an art form – they are great storytellers and are not without humour. Anglo-Saxons and Nordics may soon begin to lose their way. As an argument develops, Hungarians begin to abandon rationality for emotion, logic for rhetoric. They are great with words, often hiding what they are really saying. Exaggeration and flamboyance creep in, mixed with stylishly delivered flattery. Their natural easy-going approach can quickly switch to criticism, however. They are accomplished complainers. Pessimism, suddenly introduced, can also be distracting. Turn taking is problematic, with a tendency for everyone to talk at once. Choose your moment of entry carefully.

The Czech Republic

The Czechs are soft speakers who communicate in a thoughtful manner and in measured tones. Rushing headlong into discussion is not their style and rapid conclusions are rare. They often impress their interlocutors as being phlegmatic and lukewarm rather than just laid-back. Their humour is dry and black – quite unique in fact. There is the anecdote about the conversation during a high-level lunch between President Reagan, Helmut Kohl, Gorbachev and Czech President Havel. Each leader boasted about the pre-eminence of his country. Reagan and Kohl referred to the size of their economies. Gorbachev emphasised the hugeness of the Soviet Union. Havel pondered long before he replied: "Well, the Czech Republic has the world's biggest dwarfs."

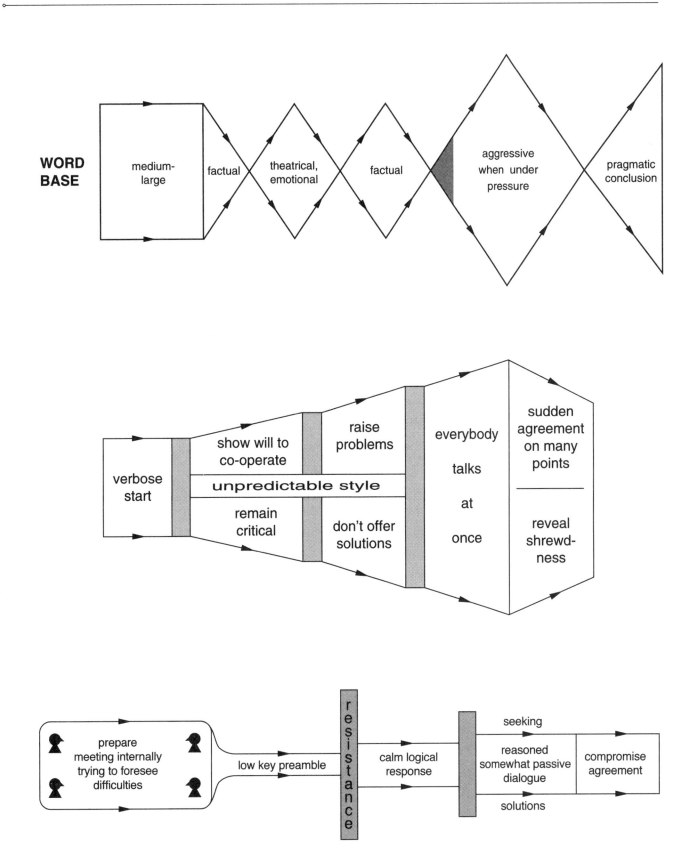

WORD BASE

medium-large | factual | theatrical, emotional | factual | aggressive when under pressure | pragmatic conclusion

verbose start | show will to co-operate | raise problems | everybody talks at once | sudden agreement on many points

unpredictable style

remain critical | don't offer solutions | reveal shrewdness

prepare meeting internally trying to foresee difficulties | low key preamble | resistance | calm logical response | seeking reasoned somewhat passive dialogue solutions | compromise agreement

Slovakia

Slovak is a kind of *lingua franca* among Slavic peoples, inasmuch as it is understandable by Czechs, Poles, Bulgarians and ex-Yugoslavs more easily than any other. This gives Slovaks considerable confidence when conversing with Slavs and they are regarded as quite loquacious and expressive in this context. When talking to West Europeans (in English or German) a certain caution creeps into their speech pattern. This is partly for linguistic reasons, but also because of oppression suffered in the past. Less reticent than Czechs, Slovaks use lengthy chunks of dialogue and though they are strong on logic, they often use charm and charisma to influence partners. There is a certain tendency to vagueness (when compared for instance with Germans) and they can often be ambiguous.

Bulgaria

In comparison with the South Slavs, Bulgarians are reticent and reserved in the early stages of acquaintance. In this they resemble the Czechs or Slovenians. Before giving full expression to their feelings or opinions, Bulgarians engage in a series of preliminary encounters where they sound out and size up (albeit in a friendly manner) their conversation partners. During this period they are decidedly less flowery or rhetorical in speech than the Yugoslavs, Romanians or Hungarians. During this stage, it is very difficult to extract opinions or eventual attitudes. When this exploratory period has passed, Bulgarians open up to display a modicum of quiet charm and make their requests in a circuitous manner, avoiding confrontation whenever they can.

Romania

Romanians are oratorical by nature (neighbours say "long-winded") and are proud of their sophistication in discourse. They rarely answer questions with "yes" or "no", so it is not advisable to ask direct questions requiring affirmative or negative answers. It is better to hint at what one wants or seeks, being prepared to read between the lines of their reply. Their answers are in any case long and complex and may to some extent reflect what you want to hear. Their delicacy is Italian in nature, as is their capacity for flexible truth when questioned aggressively. Their style of address is personal and they seek **your** opinion or support rather than that of your organisation.

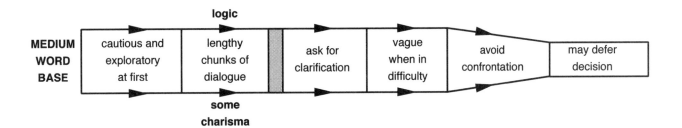

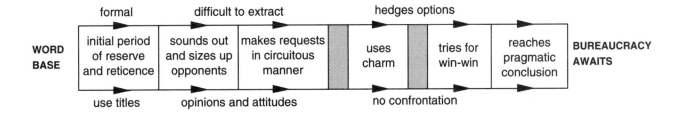

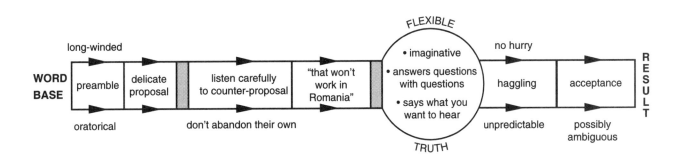

Serbia & Montenegro

Serbs can be charismatic to an extraordinary degree and present themselves well to foreigners. They are renowned for efficient lobbying, especially in the UK and USA. Social or business discussions are preceded by extensive small talk. Politics is a favourite subject. Serbs are an outspoken people, unafraid to voice their strong opinions in politics or business. In order to support their arguments, it is not unknown for them to exaggerate facts and invent some others. It is advisable to take what they say with a pinch of salt. Boasting is common (Serbs do not see anything wrong with it). However they accompany their boasts with charming anecdotes. They are good at speedy repartee, but often make contradictory statements. They are practised complainers and are quick to exploit what they see as weakness in others. Firmness and strict adherence to facts and figures are the only remedies for dealing with them. They can be extremely generous on occasion. It is advisable to ask oneself why.

Slovenia

Slovenes are not particularly talkative people (other former Yugoslavs often found them dull or boring). They resemble Western Austrians in their factuality, Czechs in their thoughtful manner and measured tones. They rarely rush headlong into discussion and are reluctant to draw rapid conclusions. The speech style is much less loquacious and emotional than those of other South Slavs. Many interlocutors find them phlegmatic and lukewarm.

Croatia

Croats possess strong opinions especially in the political sphere, but also concerning social and business matters. They are somewhat restrained in expressing them, however, and are less open than the Serbs, who often demonstrate their views forcibly or even in a fiery manner. A high level of education often enables Croats to pursue their argument in a sophisticated style. Their linguistic skills are considerable. They shun rhetoric, choosing their words carefully for best effect.

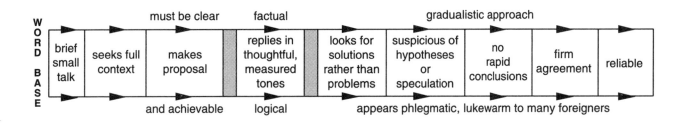

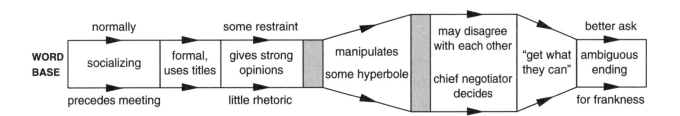

Russia

Russians are eloquent communicators and warm. They consider themselves very human and understanding and believe they can help others towards understanding and harmony. Their argument is roundabout, exploratory and indulges frequently in sentiment. Subjectivity has priority over objectivity. They can be poetic, and are aware of their great literary tradition. The level of English and other languages is surprisingly high. Circular style of discourse often confuses Westerners. Russians convey feeling well, but are not high on clarity.

Ukraine

The Ukrainian communication pattern resembles the Russian in that it is rambling, wordy, emotional and somewhat unpredictable. Western Europeans and Americans may find unusual reactions to their own advances. Ukrainian pronouncements, including business decisions, are currently coloured by political opinions – there is a serious cultural divide between East and West Ukraine. Foreign interlocutors should bear this in mind. All Ukrainians, after an initial display of warmth and hospitality, pursue a tough negotiating style typified by caution, tenacity, obstinacy and a win-lose mentality.

Belarus

In a period of history which includes the break-up of the Soviet Union, Belarus' exit from it and subsequent internal political dissension and dictatorship, Belarusians are cautious interlocutors who wish to seek solid personal relationships before "baring their soul". Conversations and negotiations are consequently preceded by long preambles, perhaps also socialising before getting down to brass tacks. Even then proposals may well be guarded, with high context inferences along the way. In later stages of discussion, agendas may be thrown to the wind and many people may talk over each other. Belarusians frequently prefer the "real deal" to be concluded in a private setting.

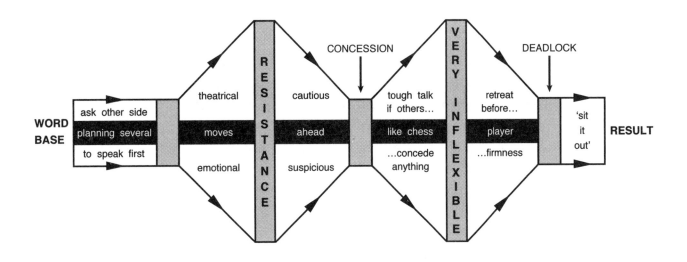

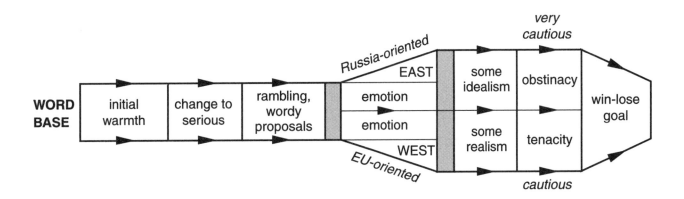

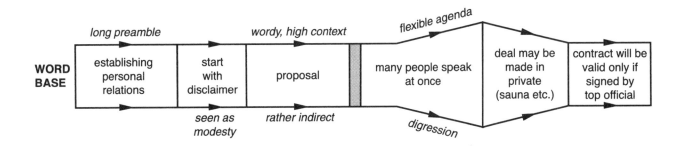

Turkey

The Turkish communication style derives from its three major roots – Islamic, Mediterranean and Eastern (Ottoman, Seljuk). The first two are sources of their liveliness – they are in the main both multi-active and dialogue-oriented. The third (Eastern) strand is, however, clearly visible – they are more reactive than any Europeans, except perhaps the Finns. Reactive cultures let the other side speak first and slowly try to modify their reply or position to fit in with their interlocutor. Given their reputation for ferocity and political obduracy, it is remarkable how controlled, reasonable and receptive Turks can be during discussion. In business circles their style is exploratory – they are very interested in all forms of change which lead to progress. They are polite and courteous (more than Westerners), but they wish to be seen as Western and modern. They show natural exasperation at being rejected by the West, but they are patient and persistent in trying to open and maintain acceptable communication channels.

Iran

Iranians are talkative (although they appear taciturn to their more talkative neighbours), but respect dignity and seriousnesss of intent in speech. They can be loquacious, but are not idle chatterers, particularly in business. They have a strong sense of what is appropriate and courteous according to context. They are keen to draw contrasts between what is proper in polite society, and what is suitable for the marketplace. They can be persuasive and admire persuasiveness in others. They can tolerate small talk, particularly mutual praise of the hospitality of others, but they soon wish to turn to the heart of the matter, to show they have a sharp intellect and to demonstrate they have something to say.

Israel

Israelis are bold and direct in conversation – they fancy themselves as US-style straight talkers in what they see as a devious Middle Eastern cultural environment. In fact many Anglo-Saxons might find them manipulative and transparently persuasive, though they stick to facts on the whole. They are argumentative, back up their opinions with logic and erudition and do not concede their positions easily. The hard school of experience has engendered not a little irony and cynicism. They are not without humour but are generally earnest and serious. Their critics would call them pushy and brash. Subtlety is not their strong point.

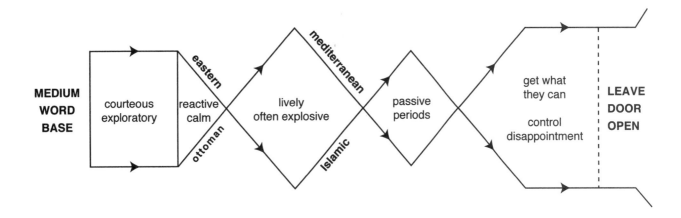

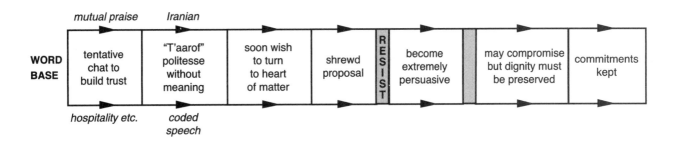

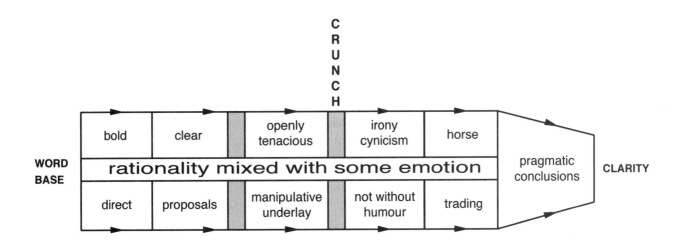

Iraq

Like most Arabs, Iraqis have a theatrical, declamatory communication style. This has been intensified on account of wartime hardship and recent suffering. In ancient times, Iraqis and Mesopotamians were not among the most xenophobic people in the Middle East. Their proud and ancient history had a legacy of eloquence and dignified pronouncement. Now plaintiveness characterises their speech, which is increasingly anti-foreign and highly moralistic.

Egypt

Extrovert, dramatic, declamatory. Eloquence is admired and expected. Reticence on your part will worry them. Arguments and business in general are highly personalized. Egyptians talk about family influence and connections in a boastful manner. They cannot refuse you a favour, but you cannot refuse their requests if you are considered a friend. Hard bargainers, Egyptians pride themselves on being able to find accommodations with Westerners, whom they feel they know well. In general they are amenable, particularly if they perceive the other side as being sincere.

Arab countries (in general)

Extremely extrovert, theatrical, declamatory. Loudness of voice indicates sincerity. Rhetoric is admired and expected. Quietness on your part will cause preoccupation. Arguments and business in general are highly personalized. Arabs talk about family influence and connections in a boastful manner. Tone of conversation is often moralistic and integrity has priority over rationality. Oaths are not uncommon – they are a feature of Arabic. One-to-one meetings are hard to come by in the Arab world, where a retinue or number of individuals share the "open office" of a VIP. Senior Arabs, though benign, often adopt a moralistic tone to younger Westerners, also to other Arabs. When their proposals are opposed, they become rhetorical and eyes can flash with passion or anger.

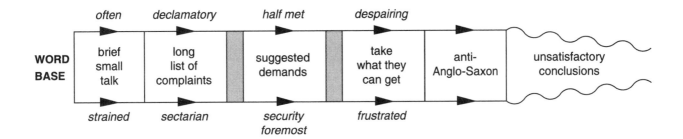

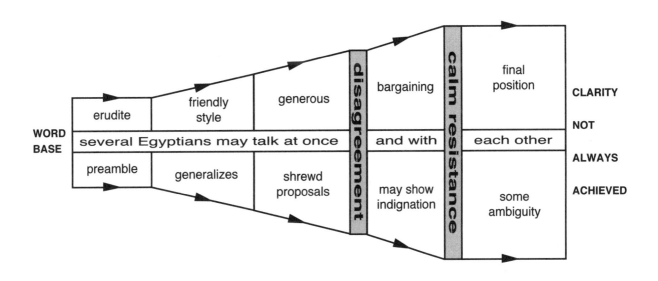

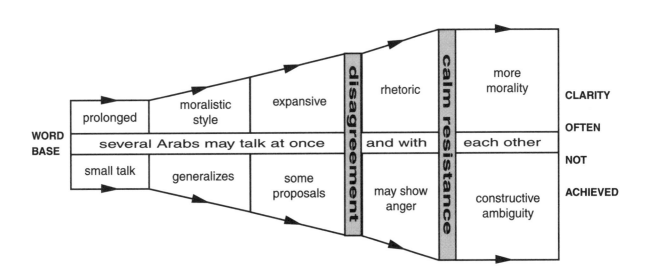

Central Asia
Azerbaijan, Kazakhstan, Uzbekistan, Kyrgyzstan, Tajikistan, Turkmenistan

The Central Asian speech pattern is basically loquacious, excitable and tough and displays a keen business sense during negotiations, especially in Uzbekistan. Uzbeks are generally considered the most commercially-minded in the area and are seen as pushy by most of their neighbours. Though multi-active on the surface, there is a definite reactive streak in Central Asian behaviour. Capable of fierceness, people tend to look before they leap, considering the pros and cons of actions relating to their neighbours. Islamic tenets and a high moral tone are also typical of their discourse.

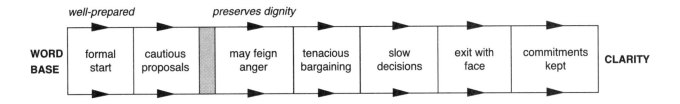

WORD BASE | *well-prepared* | *preserves dignity* | **CLARITY**

| formal start | cautious proposals | | may feign anger | tenacious bargaining | slow decisions | exit with face | commitments kept |

Kazakhstan

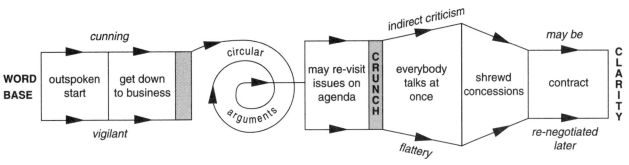

WORD BASE | *cunning* / *vigilant* | outspoken start | get down to business | *circular arguments* | may re-visit issues on agenda | **CRUNCH** | *indirect criticism* / *flattery* everybody talks at once | shrewd concessions | *may be* / *re-negotiated later* contract | **CLARITY**

Uzbekistan

India

Communication is invariably courteous in the extreme with lengthy and amiable small talk preceding getting down to business. When business is ultimately discussed, the reactive side of Indians' nature is revealed in their request to hear the other side's view first. Their (multi-active) loquacity is held in check while the other speaks. Initial reaction usually seems favourable, but Indians have the ability to modify and re-package skilfully as they work their way towards a mutually accepted agreement.

Pakistan

The Pakistani communication style is very similar to the Indian. The preamble is usually courteous with lengthy small talk. Their (multi-active) loquacity is held in check while the other speaks. Initial reaction usually seems favourable, but Pakistanis have the ability to modify and re-package skilfully as they work their way towards a mutually accepted agreement. Islamic defensiveness often surfaces. In general, they are somewhat more fiery than Indians.

Bangladesh

Foreign visitors to Bangladesh often find the people somewhat abrupt and unsophisticated in their opening conversation exchanges. This feature probably derives from the rural traditions and character of many people. They quickly warm to a foreigner who shows them some empathy and subsequently can be extremely helpful and hospitable almost to the point of embarrassment. Their traditional interest in poetry and literature makes Bangladeshis eloquent and at times oratorical. They tend to avoid strongly-worded statements or affirmations, preferring to indicate their opinions in an indirect and rather pleasant manner. They are inclined to find solutions through compromise on most matters. They are uncomfortable with silence, filling in gaps in the conversation with pleasantries.

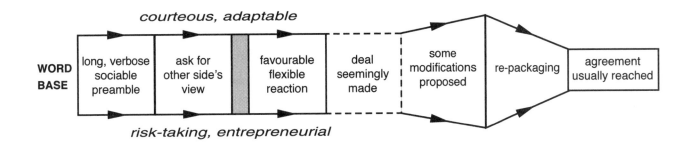

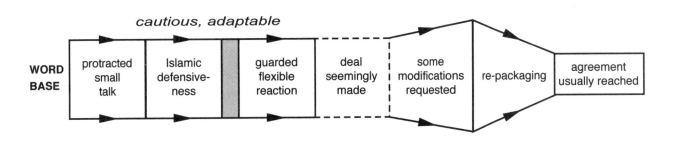

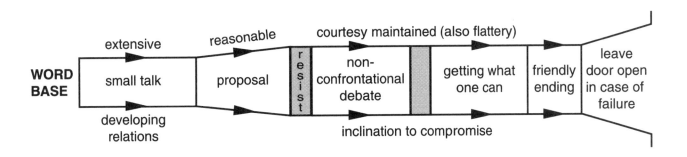

Japan

Japanese is rather a vague language and the impersonalisation of the verb combined with the complex system of honorifics can sometimes result in a certain ambiguity. There are established phrases to be used on specific occasions, and meaning is often hinted at instead of stated directly. The **manner** of speaking is more important and Japanese can create a very harmonious atmosphere with a very small number of words. When asked a question, Japanese rarely launch into an immediate answer. As a reactive culture, they wish to evaluate the implications of the question carefully and think about their response.

China

Courteous, patient discourse, generally indicating great humility and understanding. Chinese are more explicit and less introverted than the Japanese, having been more in contact with Westerners in the 19th and early 20th centuries. Chinese attend meetings in sizeable numbers and negotiate collectively. The problem for Westerners is that there is generally some state involvement and the real decision-makers are not actually in the meetings. Patient and courteous discussion is normal, but a frequent tactic is "tough talk" in fits and starts. Everyone protects everyone's face, though the Chinese often moralise about Western decadence.

Hong Kong

People in Hong Kong speak faster than Chinese mainlanders and wish to conclude deals and negotiations faster. When dealing with foreigners, their communication style is more Western than Asian. They are adept at being very direct, but saving face at the same time.

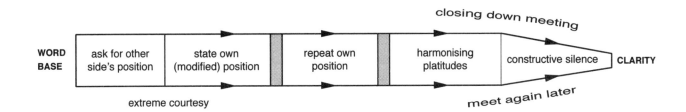

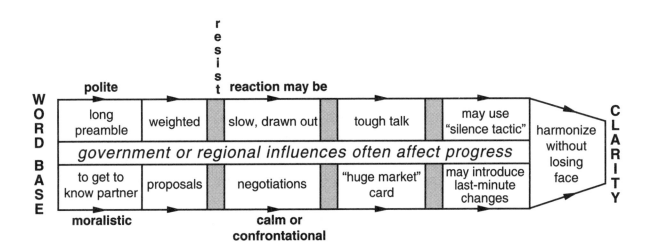

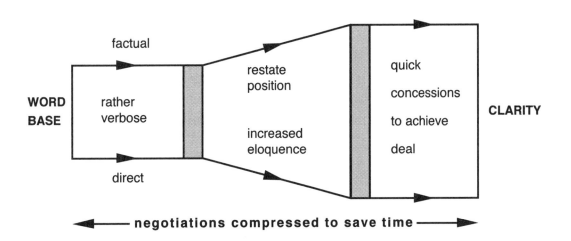

South Korea

Koreans are energetic conversationalists – very intense when serious, occasionally displaying Western-style humour when trying to charm. In Korea truth is elastic. Varieties of truth include: relative truth; only good news; what they think you want to hear; what they would like to be true; what they think has a chance to be true; what is temporarily true. Koreans believe they can handle Westerners better than other Asians can and often try their hand at humour. It is advisable to double check anything that is promised. They often are looking for quick profits and one should be careful about granting exclusivity. It is better to judge their statements against past performance rather than future forecasts.

North Korea

Talking to and negotiating with North Koreans can be a thankless and often fruitless exercise. From the outset cold and factual, North Koreans can be openly adversarial early on in the discussion. Obliged by Asian traditions to show a minimum of courtesy, they break into diatribes on the grounds that the other side has double standards, is corrupt and seeks to exploit them. All business discussion is conducted in the context of the current political situation and they make it clear that progress is to be made only on their terms. They often leave the door half open, but are rarely the first to propose further meetings.

The Philippines

Filipinos' dialogue-oriented, rather emotional communication somewhat resembles Spanish, but is less forceful and exuberant. Oratory is valued and speeches can be lengthy. Though Tagalog is used throughout the country, the Philippines is, at a functional level, the second-largest English-speaking nation in the world.

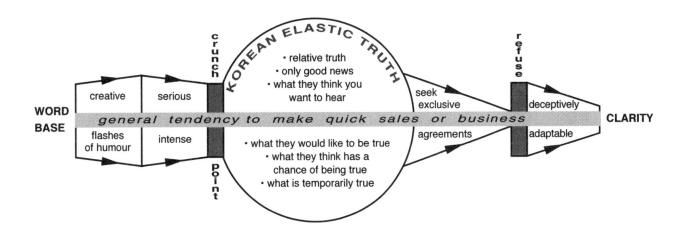

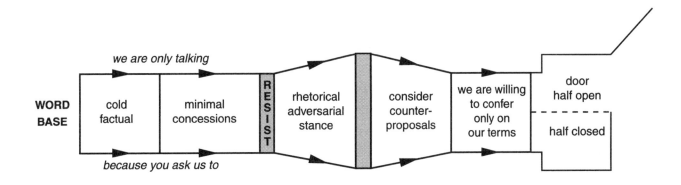

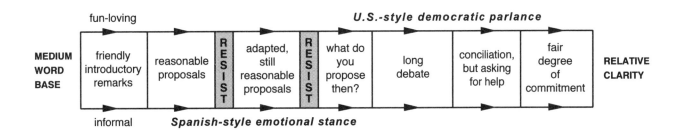

Thailand

People who keep cool are respected and it is considered appropriate to smile even (and especially) in stressful situations. Buddhist moderation is the rule and if one is angered and seeks revenge it must be obtained by subtle methods. Frankness is not highly valued and unpleasant truths are avoided. Only about 20% of one's personal problems will be spelled out. Some hypocrisy is not considered negative. Humour (largely puns) is fairly frequent.

Vietnam

French influence is readily observable. Facial expression is much more evident than in, for instance, Japan, Korea or China and some body language reminiscent of the French is to be seen. Emotional factors can be used in argument. Good education and a high rate of literacy lend people confidence in communication. The literary tradition is strong, particularly in poetry. People in the South tend to be more open and frank than many Asians (no doubt due to prolonged contact with the Americans).

Myanmar

The Burmese communication style is typically south-east Asian in its gentleness and diffidence, but more guarded than Malaysian or Indonesian in view of the political snooping existing at all levels of society. Statements are guided by the tenets of Theravada Buddhism; humour is always just beneath the surface. Burmese, in fact, just love to laugh. Conversations and negotiations with state employees and officials are monitored by the military and are unsatisfactory in terms of getting to grips with the intrinsically charming Burmese persona.

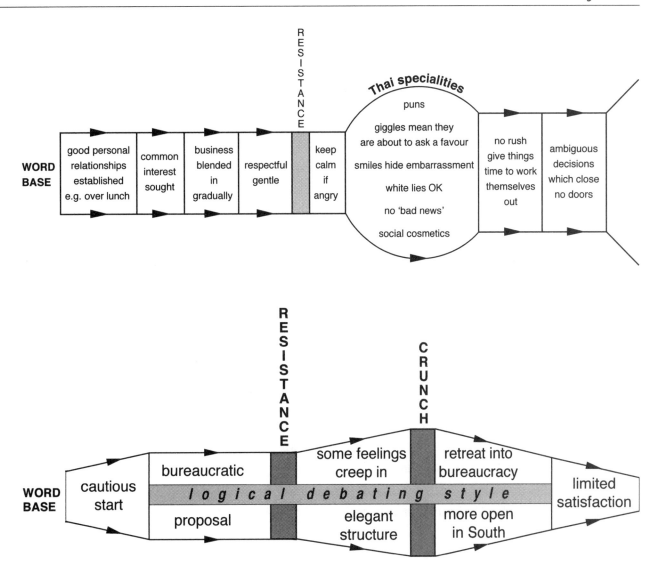

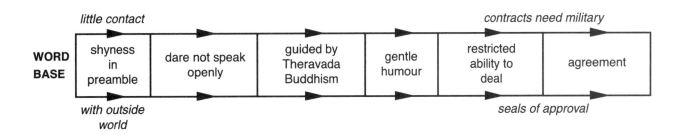

Singapore

Courteous, patient discourse, generally indicating great humility and understanding. Singaporeans are more explicit and less introverted than the Japanese, having been more in contact with Westerners in the 19th and early 20th centuries. They are very skilled negotiators.

Indonesia

Communication is dialogue-oriented, loquacious, but conducted in a quiet voice and without displaying intensity of emotion. Confrontation is avoided and problems or areas of difference are alluded to in an indirect manner. They also are reluctant to admit they don't know the answer to a question. They often give wrong directions! Indonesians excel in respect language and, in the reactive manner, modify their own proposals out of deference. They are clever at saying what you want to hear. They can engage in prolonged, childlike questioning to clarify intent, though meetings often end with a few loose ends floating around. They can be tantalisingly ambiguous.

Malaysia

The Malaysian communication pattern is very similar to the Indonesian. It is dialogue-oriented, loquacious, but conducted in a quiet voice and without displaying intensity of emotion. Confrontation is avoided and problems or areas of difference are alluded to in an indirect manner. They also are reluctant to admit they don't know the answer to a question. Some British influence is evident in debating. Communication is formal at first, with gradual informality being introduced over time. They usually speak excellent English.

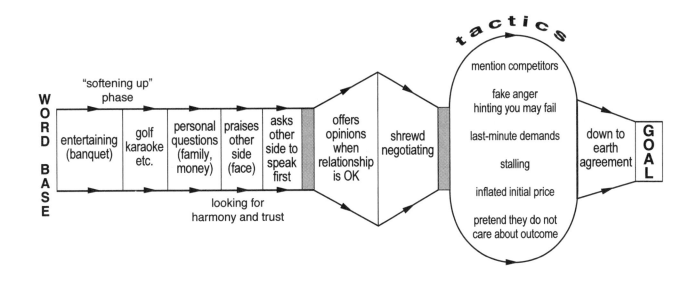

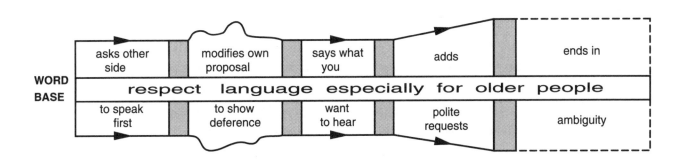

British debating style

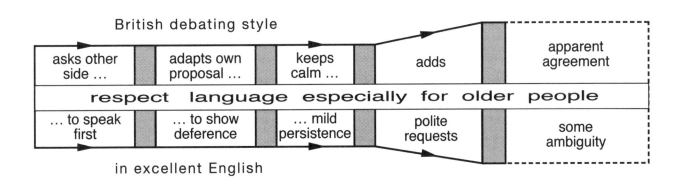

in excellent English

French North Africa

Algerians, Tunisians and Moroccans all share an eloquent, passionate communication pattern which benefits from Arab and Berber rhetoric, French oratory and rationality and a firm belief in the positive elements of their glorious cultured past, when they inspired a shining multi-cultural civilisation in Andalucía and round the Mediterranean shores. North Africans are shrewd bargainers and negotiators, but often emanate warmth and generosity in solutions, though they seem to pursue win-lose in their favour. Their Islamic beliefs and pronouncements are tempered by their familiarity with Western concepts and practices, especially French ones. They are tolerant of other views and rely mainly on logic to find solutions. Their shows of anger and passion are sometimes feigned.

Portuguese Africa

African warmth and rhetoric combine with Portuguese-influenced loquacity and argumentation to produce a distinct communication pattern in Angola and Mozambique. A long, socialising preamble eases gently into an often unrealistic proposal, where speakers are "testing the water". Resistance to the proposal can produce a somewhat naïve "why not?" reaction, which has to be dealt with in a patient manner. Agendas are not adhered to very carefully and various digressions can often introduce quite wild and unviable ideas which were not part of the original context of the discussion. These can generally be reined in. Speakers with Portuguese education can be steered by logical argument.

Sub-Saharan Africa

African communication is at the outset warm and friendly and in many cases is couched in poetic and symbolistic terms. Colour, charisma and rhetoric come naturally to Africans, naturally enhanced by improved education. When conducting a business meeting, warmth is tempered by tenacity in defending tribal interest. For the African, communication is a vital process, since Africans, like Japanese, Chinese and Mexicans among others, believe that a person is not a person unless they have someone they can communicate with.

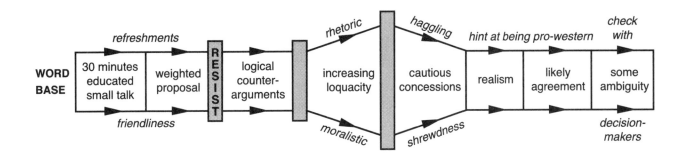

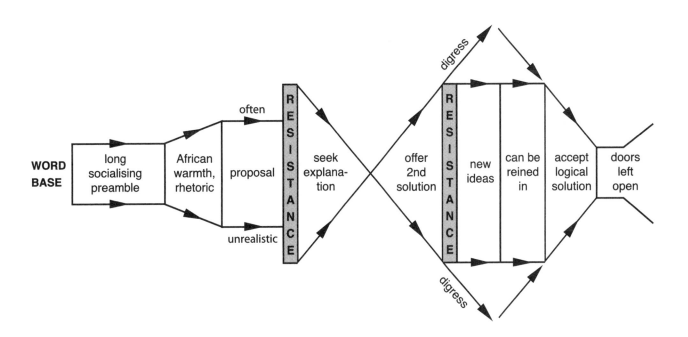

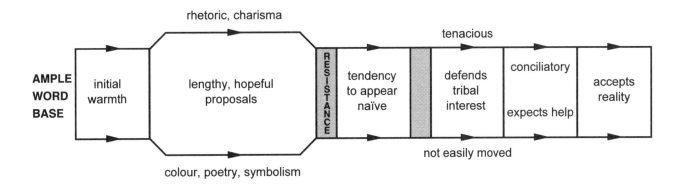

South Africa (black)

Black South Africans are not unused to dealing and negotiating with whites, albeit experience gained in a less friendly era. Accordingly they expect absolutely equal treatment from the outset, now the shoe is on the other foot. Familiarity with white negotiating methods stands them in good stead. Following Mandela's example, they strive to maintain a meaningful dialogue with whites. Some resentment and impatience show through, initial proposals are weighted and bargaining can be prolonged. Nevertheless, business gets done in a pragmatic manner.

South Africa (white British)

British South Africans are often more expressive than Britons in speech and have a well-articulated and rather pleasing English accent. They tend to avoid aggressive or impolite forms. Like southern English people, they use some coded speech.

South Africa (white Dutch)

Afrikaners have a distinct accent, are blunter in expression, but are generally clear and analytical. There is little deviousness and coded speech is almost unknown to them.

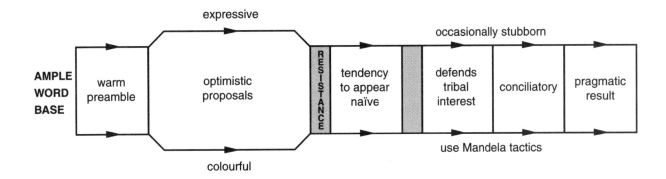

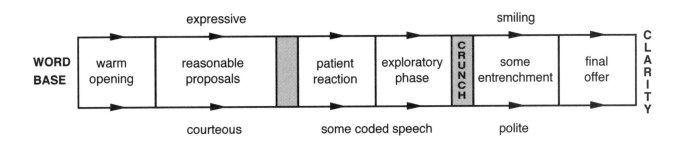

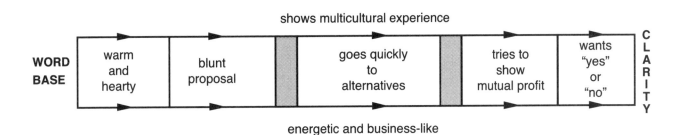

Australia

Australian meetings are in the main relatively informal affairs, beginning with cups of tea and first names and ending in compromise where everyone feels he/she has taken away something. In between, exchanges can be lively, blunt, cynical, even aggressive, though in general the participants are looking for solutions. With foreigners, Australians make efforts to curb their national irreverence for superiors and institutions.

New Zealand

The New Zealand communication style is not unlike that of the (southern) English, but less enigmatic or coded and with a refreshing "rural" straightforwardness. They are conservative and cautious by nature, but handle language well and quickly gain trust from their interlocutors. When challenged, they remain calm at all times and are surprisingly innovative and sharp-eyed under their laid-back veneer.

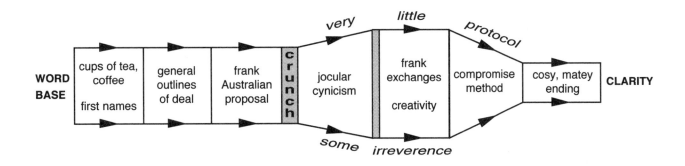

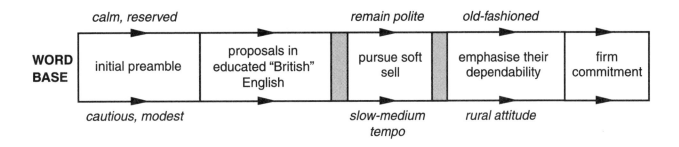

USA

In the USA one puts one's cards on the table at the beginning and spells it all out again in louder English for foreigners who hesitate. When Americans feel they are getting bogged down, they use sarcasm and provocative measures to get the meeting going. For them a real fight is communication. Amongst themselves, they push the other side to the limit and then make quick, mutual concessions to make sure the deal goes through. Formal negotiators such as French, Germans and Japanese find this style somewhat disconcerting.

Canada

Canadian English sounds pleasing to most ears, being measured, well-articulated and lacking the extreme nasal tones of some US accents. This calm delivery, allied to a generally reasonable manner, enables Canadians to create a positive impression with people who don't understand English! French Canadians possess more Gallic fervour, but in fact are much more Anglicised (linguistically) than they would care to admit and are less roundabout and loquacious than European French.

Mexico

Scandinavians, Japanese and some other reticent peoples often convey their thoughts and values through quiet, reliable actions. Mexicans prefer words. Of all the varieties of Spanish, Mexican, with its abundant use of diminutives and colourful imagery, is perhaps the most flowery. Like Italians, they leave little unsaid, are generous in their praise and flattery and when talking to foreigners, rarely say anything that you do not want to hear. In Mexico people are expected to discuss issues at length, seeking the agreement or conversion of the other and leaving no stone unturned to make oneself clear. As with most Latins, conversation is regarded as an art and they fully expect you as their partner to give as good as you get.

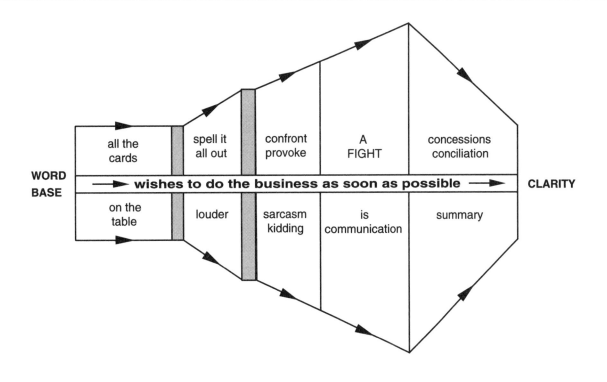

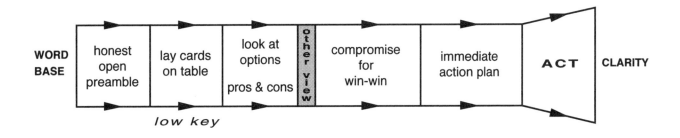

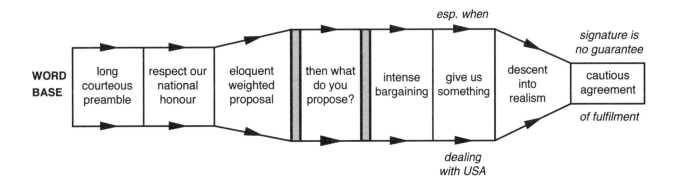

Hispanic America (in general)

Meetings with Hispanic Americans are more complicated than with say Nordics or Australians. To begin with a lot of small talk is expected and Americans and Northern Europeans would have to give clear signs of respecting the national honour of their counterparts. Initial proposals are often far removed from realistic conclusions and protracted haggling is part of the process. Agreements reached are often somewhat inconclusive and strict adherence to contract is questionable.

Brazil

Loquacious in the extreme, the Brazilians use gestures and facial expressions to emphasise their point of view. Although appearing over-emotional at times, they only intend for you to understand that what they are saying "comes from the heart." The more lengthy their discourse, the more they feel they will have cemented your loyalty, as a basis on which they can build further transactions and create long-term goodwill. In Brazil, meetings are extremely verbose and human feelings take precedence over close examination of the facts. Brazilians are rarely the bearers of bad news and a certain amount of healthy scepticism is advisable. Leisurely haggling often leads to satisfactory agreements, though it is as well to summarize carefully what all parties are supposed to do.

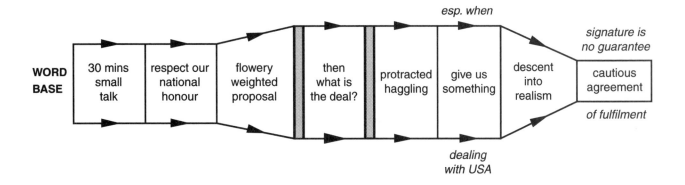

WORD BASE → 30 mins small talk → respect our national honour → flowery weighted proposal → then what is the deal? → protracted haggling → give us something → descent into realism → cautious agreement

esp. when → *signature is no guarantee*

dealing with USA → *of fulfilment*

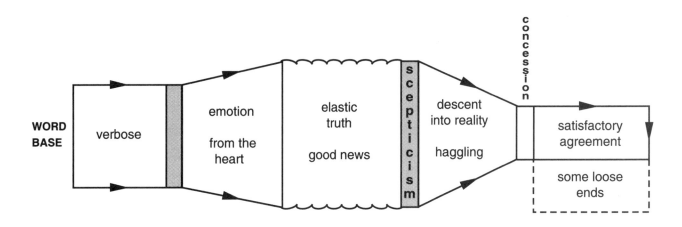

WORD BASE → verbose → emotion / from the heart → elastic truth / good news → scepticism → descent into reality / haggling → concession → satisfactory agreement / some loose ends

Cuba

The Cuban communication pattern, inherited basically from Spain, has numerous African overtones in terms of warmth, colour and spontaneity. Business discussions are lively, often with several people talking at once. Decisions are made in conformity with the policies of the current Castroite regime and pronouncements are by necessity usually guarded. Within these constraints, kindliness and hospitality show through.

Jamaica

Jamaicans tend to be assertive in meetings, with strong eye contact, direct approach and colourful, powerful language. They use a rather high pitch tone and like to gesticulate freely. They love drama. When negotiating, they make a point of coming to the meeting very well prepared. They like to draw from past experiences and attach great importance to feasibility studies. They are good at developing future scenarios which benefit them and are used to long meetings. They are often the last to concede in negotiations. Written contracts are not taken too seriously.

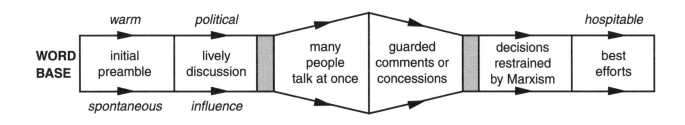

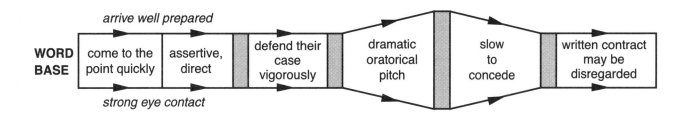

Exercises

1 | What is your own communication pattern like? Describe it briefly in words below:

-
-
-
-
-
-
-

2 | Now draw a diagram to describe your communication pattern in the space below, combining words and visuals:

3 Flick through the communication pattern diagrams on pages 3-55. Which cultures are you most similar to and which ones do you differ from? Write them down below:

Similar

Different

-
-
-
-
-

4 Think about colleagues, clients and friends from other cultures. Which ones do you communicate with easily, and which ones do you sometimes have trouble with?

Easy communication

Difficult communication

-
-
-
-
-

5 Is a particular communication issue causing you problems at the moment?
Visit **www.crossculture.com/visualapproach**, describe your situation, and we will try to help.

6 If you wish to find out more about your own personal communication pattern and how it compares to over 80 other cultures – e.g. to help improve communication with colleagues, clients and friends – visit **www.cultureactive.com** and try the online cultural assessment.

Listening Habits

Captive audiences generally appear to listen, but in fact they listen to different degrees and in different ways. There are good listeners and bad listeners. Others, such as the Americans, listen carefully or indifferently, depending on the nature of the address.

Although each nationality has its own specific style of listening, one can divide them into rough categories, where certain generalisations apply. For instance Nordics (Danes, Finns, Norwegians and Swedes) could readily be described as the best listeners, partly because their own natural reticence gives them no incentive to interrupt. Calm concentration is a strong point.

Germanic peoples are also good listeners. Both Germans and Dutch are hungry for the facts, though the latter wish to start a debate fairly soon. Disciplined Germans have perhaps the longest attention span of any nationality, diligently making notes as they listen.

As far as the Anglo-Saxons are concerned, English and Canadians pay polite attention as long as the speaker is reasonably low key. Debate is required afterwards. Australians are more cynical and can't take too much seriousness, but, like Americans, will listen well if technical information is being imparted. Americans, used to show business and encapsulated news items, tend to lose concentration if they are not entertained in some way.

In ex-Communist countries, e.g. Russia, Poland and the Baltic states, listening habits are directly and strongly affected by previous and recent political control (propaganda). Most Eastern Europeans believe all official statements are lies and that any changes introduced by the authorities are for the worse. Speakers must therefore combat automatic scepticism in these cultures. This is compounded in Russia by an inherent suspicion of foreigners. Hungarians tend to be less apathetic than some of the others.

Countries which have had a colonial past – India, Malaysia, Indonesia – also listen with a certain amount of suspicion, though they can be won over by an eloquent and thoroughly respectful speaker. Reaction is, however, deceptive, since listeners in these areas give feedback which they think will please. They also are reluctant to admit to gaps in comprehension.

As we go further east, the Confucian cultures of China, Japan and Korea have language problems and are also reluctant to confess to non-comprehension. What they listen for principally is exaggerated respect from the speaker, so that nobody loses face. Chinese and Koreans are traditionally suspicious of Westerners. The Japanese are more open to address, but so involved with politeness and vague expressions that messages often do not get across.

Latins are not very attentive listeners in principle, as they are normally anxious to speak themselves. A charismatic speaker may hold them for 30 minutes or more, but the French in particular do not believe that foreigners can teach them very much. Italians have busy minds and wander.

Spaniards dislike monologues – they want to interject and argue vigorously. Latin Americans show interest in new ideas, but are somewhat sceptical about European caution and even more so about US exploitation.

Arabs are not good listeners when they are in groups, though they like an extra talk afterwards in private. They are defensive about Islam.

Africans listen respectfully in order to learn and acquire know-how, though they need to have things spelled out slowly and tend to be fatalistic about outcomes.

All in all, it is advisable for speakers, salesmen, presenters, etc., to familiarize themselves as much as possible in advance with the traditional expectations of the audience to be addressed. Style and content should be adapted accordingly.

England

The English, with their debating traditions, must listen well in order to construct their reply. Polite listening is mandatory, though one may occasionally interrupt. English speakers would normally be rather understated and include humour, so foreign speakers would do well to follow suit. Feedback is often lively and productive.

Scotland

Scots are cautious, but alert listeners who pride themselves on rarely missing a trick. Constantly thrifty, they generally focus on the bottom line, but are listening for win-win indications and give good, honest feedback. It is almost impossible to "pull the wool over Scots' eyes". They rarely interrupt speakers and give them the time they need to express their ideas. They react better to foreign speakers than do the English.

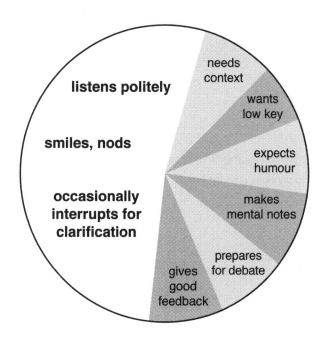

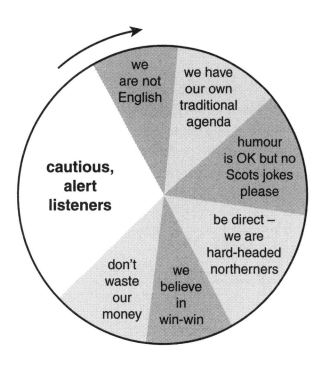

Ireland

When listening, the Irish are courteous and attentive and rarely show open dissent. They often have a strong desire to interrupt (as they are bursting with ideas), but rarely do so. Their feedback is ample enough, but occasionally is rather ambiguous or even devious.

Wales

Welsh people like to be addressed as Welsh – not English – and consequently in a direct, almost cosy manner. It is not necessary to use coded speech for politeness (e.g. "I agree, up to a point.") – a frank answer is preferable. Humour must be part of any presentation and any form of snobbery is taboo. Welsh people listen courteously, but may engage in friendly banter if the speaker is too long-winded.

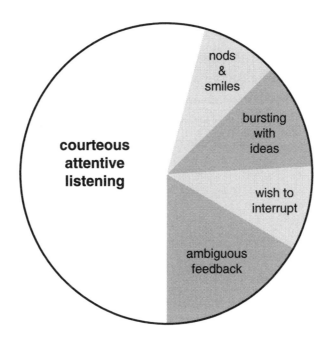

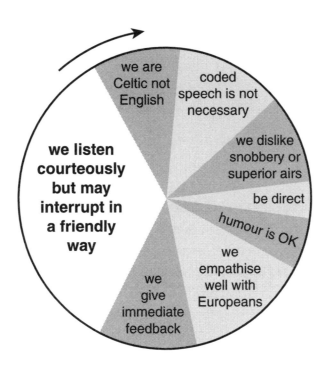

Germany

Germans listen well because they are disciplined and always willing to learn more. They have a long attention span when absorbing information and especially like repetition and plenty of background. Germans rarely expect or want to be entertained in a work context. They are serious-minded and when they hear your carefree comments, they may interpret them as important statements and ask for more information, examples or details. Simple messages sound incomplete to German ears.

Italy

Italians are sympathetic listeners, but are often restless as they "think ahead" of the speaker. Politeness prevents them from frequently interrupting, but they listen only part of the time, because they are formulating their response for when the speaker has finished. They dislike careful instructions or explanations, as they feel quite capable of understanding intuitively what messages are being conveyed. They are impatient to join the dialogue which will define the relationship between the two people.

France

French people have their own agenda and are rather poor listeners in general. They pay full attention only if the speaker is charismatic, imaginative, clearly logical and represents authority. A firm belief in their own intellectual superiority makes them reluctant to be guided by people from other cultures. The attitude is: we probably know already, French is best anyhow, we have busy minds, so say something interesting and make it quick.

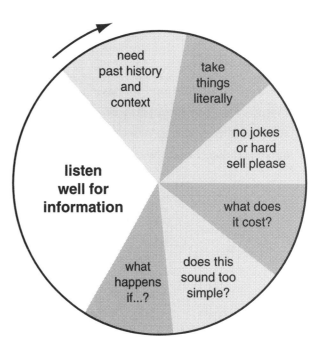

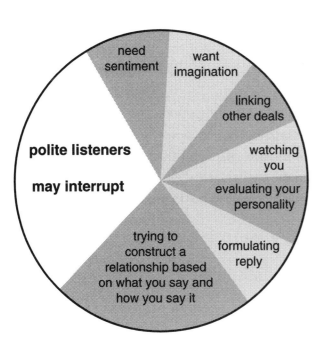

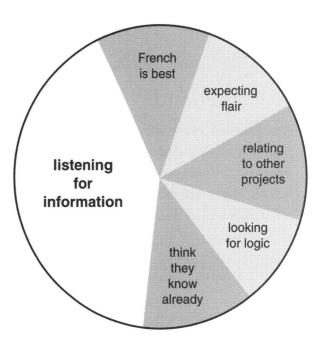

Switzerland

Swiss are good listeners, not having any great urge to expound ideas at length themselves. They forget little of what you tell them, often taking notes while you speak, and they almost never interrupt. They are conservative in their opinions and it is unlikely that they will be greatly swayed by your advice or persuasion.

Spain

Spaniards are not dedicated listeners. They read less than any other people in Europe and pay little attention to the content of presentations. They do, however, watch you carefully and sum you up by observing your physical characteristics, your mannerisms and your willingness to participate in the congenial and jocular socialising which will inevitably follow. You need to be imaginative to hold their attention for more than 20 minutes.

The Netherlands

Dutch audiences are both easy and difficult: easy in the sense that they are hungry for information and good ideas, difficult because they are very experienced and not open to much persuasion by others. Like the French, they tend to "know it all", but will in fact accept and seize viable plans and projects which are presented vigorously and backed-up with convincing evidence.

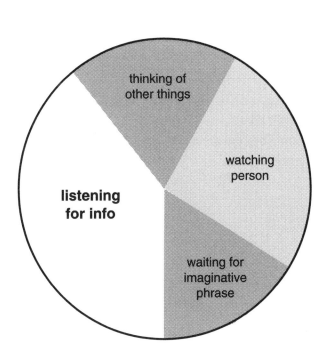

Austria (Vienna)

Austrian politeness and agreeableness make them attentive listeners on the surface. They are, however, always anxious to speak themselves and, given the opportunity, they often take up where they left off. It is common for them to resume with "Yes, but..."

Austria (Tirol)

Tirolean Austrians are more Germanic and less devious than Viennese. Often rustic in character, they want hard facts and reliable information. They are pleasant enough, but do not give too much feedback. Good attention span.

Portugal

The Portuguese are good listeners at middle class level, though upper classes tend to follow their own silent agenda while apparently listening solicitously. They are good at gathering information and don't miss much. They try to anticipate difficulties and plan much more carefully than, for instance, Spaniards. They are more international in outlook than other Latins and have better comprehension of English. They also have little difficulty in following Spanish or French.

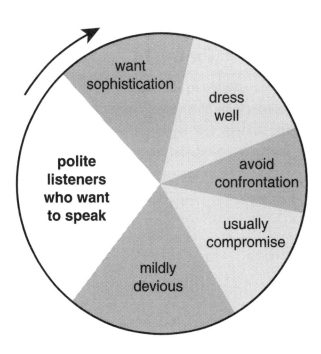

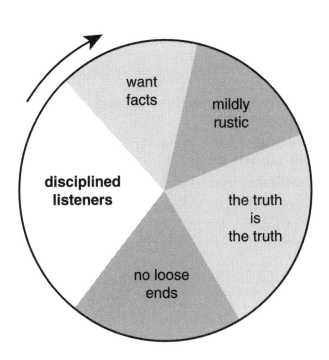

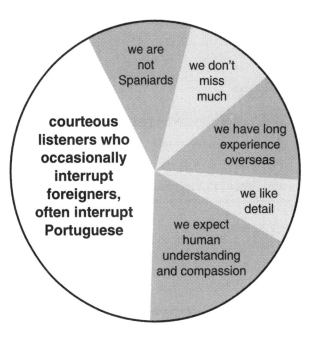

Belgium (Flemish)

Flemings listen to each other "in a circle". They are attentive, as the end result is likely to be an amalgamation of all ideas put forward. Everyone should know the strategy. Like Swedes, they want consensus. A low key presentation, using understatement and willingness to compromise goes down well.

Belgium (Walloon)

Meetings are for briefing, so that subordinates tend to listen to superiors rather than the other way round. Staff don't always know what the strategy is. Walloon managers handle foreign audiences skilfully, treading carefully. Speakers should appear authoritative, but somewhat cautious, and willing to settle for a gradualist approach.

Greece

Greeks are good listeners, since they wish to be well-informed about business. As they are very imaginative, they tend, however, to interrelate the subject under discussion with other matters. Speakers should adopt a personal style and look the Greeks in the eye when addressing them.

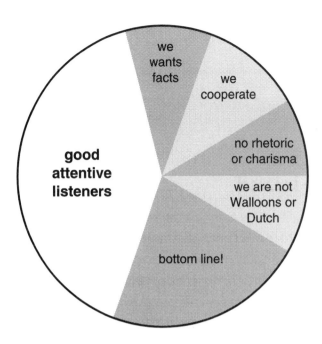

good
attentive
listeners

we
wants
facts

we
cooperate

no rhetoric
or charisma

we are not
Walloons or
Dutch

bottom line!

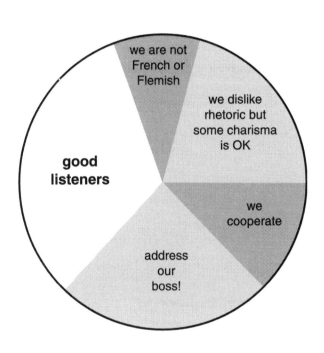

good
listeners

we are not
French or
Flemish

we dislike
rhetoric but
some charisma
is OK

we
cooperate

address
our
boss!

listens well

wishes to
be fully
informed

strong
eye
contact

we Greeks
are
experienced

we are
sophisticated

interrelates
other
matters

show us
the way
to profit

Finland

Finns are amongst the world's best listeners and are trained not to interrupt, to respect and value each other's remarks and to give careful consideration to the opinions and proposals of others. Concentration levels are high. They may give little or no feedback to a business presentation. Amongst themselves, they often feel very little pressure to contribute actively to discussion. Active listening (showing interest and involvement in the conversation) is rare and this is often troubling to other nationalities meeting Finns.

Sweden

Swedes are co-operative listeners who give encouraging, whispered feedback during the presentation. They want facts and technical details and an enormous amount of context. As consensus is obligatory in Sweden, they are nervous about what others in the audience may be thinking. Speakers should adopt a gentle and considerate tone. Swedish listeners dislike too much speculation.

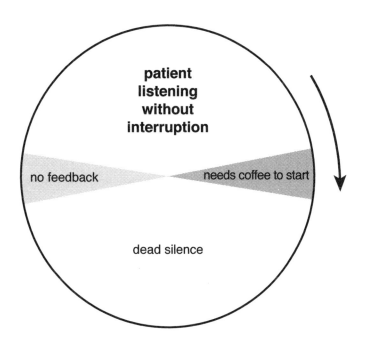

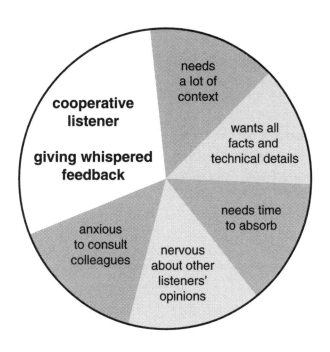

Denmark

The Danes are good listeners, who rarely interrupt, but are quite willing to ask questions afterwards. Questions are good and pertinent, showing that absorption of facts was efficient. They are skilful at establishing a meaningful dialogue. Danes make a pleasant smiling audience, but in fact hide a healthy dose of cynicism. They create counter-proposals while listening and give immediate feedback. Speakers should be modest, humorous and essentially democratic. Human rights are paramount.

Norway

Norwegians listen in good humour, but quickly develop strong opinions which they soon expose. They are data-oriented, but appreciate a personal touch. They are Norway-centred. If the speaker is not convincing enough, they will soon occupy an entrenched position. Speakers should mention Norwegian uniqueness and integrity. Also ask for their opinions early on. Beware of imposing solutions on them.

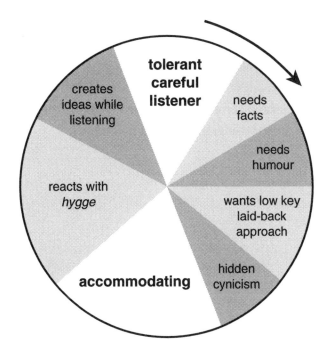

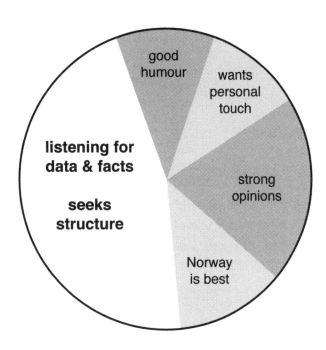

Estonia

Estonians listen quietly, give no or very little feedback or reassurance, wait for people to have their say, and then perhaps will respond. Silence can be positive as well as negative. When satisfied with the information they receive, they feel no need to gush. Americans and southern Europeans are normally disappointed at the lack of responsiveness. Finns and Swedes understand perfectly.

Latvia

Latvians are unlikely to interrupt a speaker and will listen closely. They give few clues as to what they are thinking and little feedback. Official-sounding speech makes Latvians suspicious or switches them off. They are slow to warm to strangers. It is sometimes hard to extract smiles from them.

Lithuania

Lithuanians are good and respectful listeners, though somewhat impatient if they have opinions to offer. They are quick to recognise the feelings of others. Official sounding information and opinions are likely to switch a Lithuanian listener off. When listening to a lively presentation, they show more responsiveness than Latvians, Estonians and Finns.

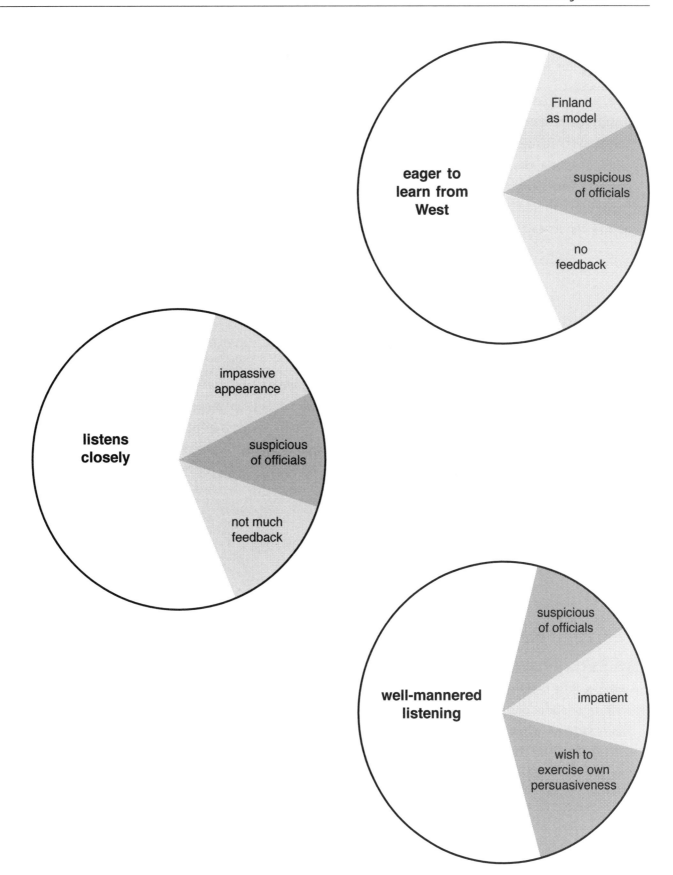

Poland

They are courteous and rarely interrupt, but listen with calm Polish scepticism and distrust to most official announcements. This last reaction is typical of the former communist regimes. They are quick to detect minor slights. The key to Polish attention is to address very personal messages and proposals to future business partners. They like visitors to refer to Polish history and achievement; ideas and suggestions should be placed in a Polish context. Though high-spirited, Poles are good listeners and restrain their desire to break in.

Hungary

Hungarians have rather complex listening habits and require various ingredients to keep their attention. Listening is problematic, as all participants are anxious to contribute the maximum rather than wait their turn. There is rapid loss of interest if conversation is not relevant. Small talk is not a prominent feature.

The Czech Republic

The Czechs are dutiful listeners, always polite and courteous. They rarely interrupt and give little feedback. As they think in linear fashion, they are uncomfortable with roundabout or digressive discussion (typical of Latins and some brother Slavs) and have a low tolerance for ambiguity. Their response, if they are unhappy, can be ironic and contain veiled sarcasm. They don't like loudness.

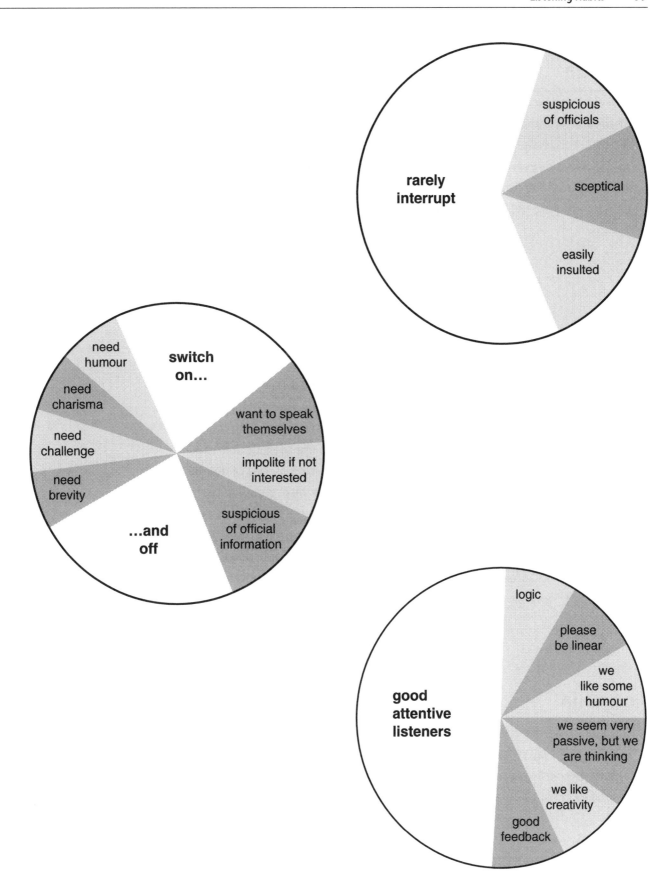

Slovakia

Slovaks listen well as they are normally polite and courteous and wish to learn. They rarely interrupt a foreigner, though they occasionally do so with other Slovaks. They have a tendency to distrust official information – a consequence of the Soviet-style years. They often ask for information to be repeated, as they wish to avoid misunderstandings. They admire daring, interesting interlocutors and get bored if they are not sufficiently entertained.

Bulgaria

Bulgarians, with no urgent desire to dominate conversation, are excellent listeners. They interrupt their compatriots rarely, foreigners hardly ever. Their attentiveness denotes their proclivity towards sizing up the speaker and dispelling their own suspicions or anxiety regarding motives. They wish to impute laudable motives, but take this step cautiously. They are not used to Western modes of discussion, so they learn as they go along. In general, they respect Western opinions, though do not always place the right connotation on what is said. They give a modicum of feedback a few minutes after absorbing a presentation or new idea. They do not reveal the full extent of their reaction – only a certain proportion. Their level of education and literacy is high, so they are capable of accurate evaluation and judgement. They can, however, be misled by Western terminology.

Romania

Romanians are attentive but suspicious listeners, who may interrupt you if anything you say strikes a discord. They are used to lengthy presentations and arguments, so if you are too brief you will not make much impact. Their feedback can be lengthy.

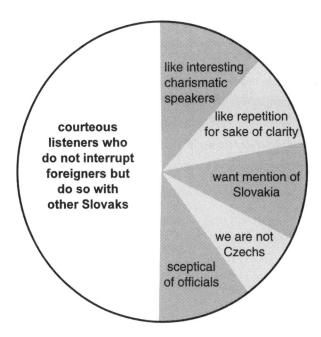

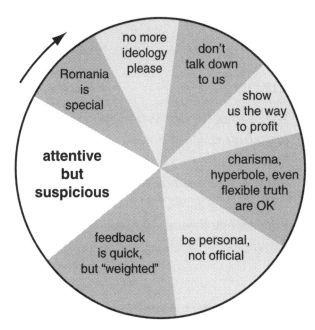

Serbia & Montenegro

They are not the world's best listeners, inasmuch as they are suspicious and lapse into cynicism easily. They are, however, swayed by sophisticated and rational discourse, especially from a Western source. They may interrupt interlocutors, but generally do so in a courteous manner. Their quick minds cause them to evaluate speakers and formulate their reply while listening.

Slovenia

Slovenes are good listeners, who remain attentive and rarely interrupt. In Yugoslav days they often felt tricked by Serbs and even Croats and consequently are on their guard against loquacious or devious speakers. Like Germans they listen for information and sieve through facts carefully. They dislike emotion or loudness and have a low tolerance for ambiguity or vagueness. They give little feedback.

Croatia

They are not the world's best listeners, inasmuch as they are suspicious of any arguments coming from an eastern direction and lapse into cynicism easily. They are, however, swayed by sophisticated and rational discourse, especially from a Western source. They may interrupt interlocutors, but generally do so in a courteous manner. Their quick minds cause them to evaluate speakers and formulate their reply while listening. Dalmatian Croats have a similar listening pattern to that of Italians. Further north they are influenced more by cold facts.

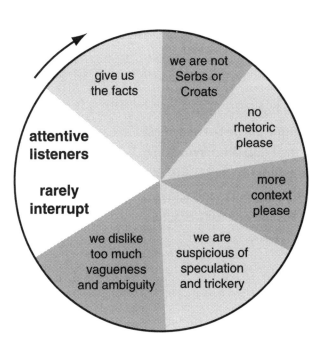

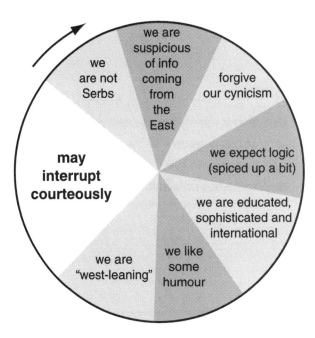

Russia

Russians automatically distrust official statements, whether made by governments, state agencies or big multinationals. Personal messages, even rumour, ring true. Russians listen best, in small numbers or privately, to a person who presents an opportunity, shares their fate and conspires to "beat the system". Speakers, especially foreigners, should be blunt, confiding and avoid any deviousness.

Ukraine

Ukrainians are patient listeners, eagerly seeking benefits, but react strongly to differences of political opinion. The current politico-cultural divide between East and West Ukraine means that speakers must allow for their Russian-orientation or their EU-orientation. In both cases Ukrainian nationalism must be respected. Less political tendencies are listeners' expectations of emotional speech, animation, some humour and kindliness towards older people. Suspicion is usually a factor.

Belarus

Listening is mainly passive, but opinions may be voiced once a certain amount of trust has entered into the relationship. Life is somewhat bleak for many Belarusians, who listen sympathetically to others' problems, but are not quick to offer remedies or solutions.

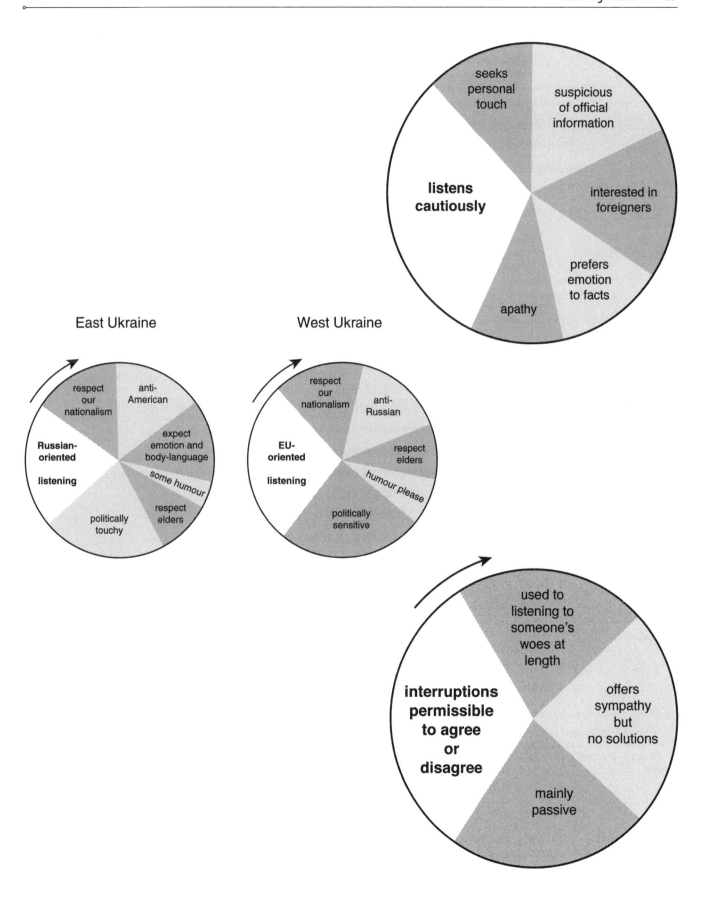

East Ukraine

West Ukraine

Turkey

As reactives, they are good listeners, wishing desperately to learn from Western colleagues. They control their Mediterranean ebullience and their Islamic righteousness to the extent that they normally refrain from interrupting their interlocutor. Neither do they try to speak over him/her in the French or Arab manner. They listen with some scepticism, but generally impute best motives and are rarely unreasonable unless they feel they are being duped.

Iran

Iranians like to talk, but they will listen attentively if they think that their interlocutor has something new to say. They are greedy for technical know-how and, because of their admiration for "experts", will listen eagerly to the latest technological ideas. However, care should be taken not to give the impression that the West is superior, as they will respond very negatively if they feel that you lack respect for or undervalue them. After all, they have a powerful sense of the superiority of their own spiritual values and wish to build a better future for themselves, through technology, without espousing values that they view as decadent and doomed to eventual failure.

Israel

Impatience and an urge to voice their opinions make them poor listeners. They often feel that foreigners cannot put themselves in Israeli shoes. They are conscious of an innate intelligence which causes them to discount many opinions of interlocutors. They can be swayed by good speakers who stick to facts and reason and who demonstrate they know something that Israelis do not know.

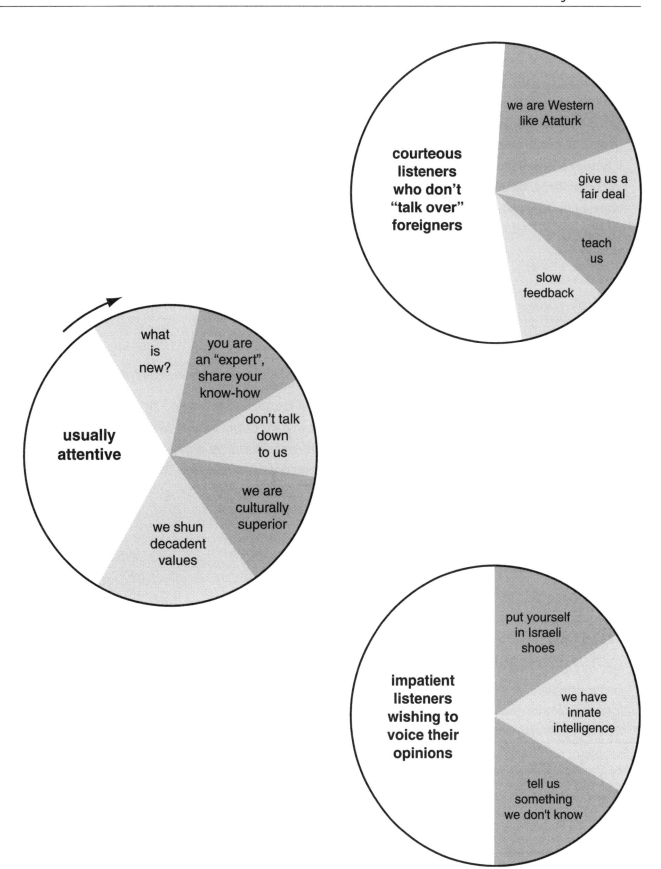

Iraq

Basically intelligent listeners, Iraqis have been sadly disillusioned by monologues and dictates of despots, clerics, Sunni, Shiite and Baathist extremists and forces of occupation. They now listen defensively and with increasing impatience. Interruptions are common and may be vehemently hostile. They are understandably desperate for good news, competence and compassion for their difficulties. Only sincere speakers who can show them ways to improve their security and well-being in general can expect a good hearing.

Egypt

Rather good listeners, but wish to speak themselves. General hubbub in an Egyptian house/office makes careful listening difficult. A less than charismatic speaker may find they talk while he/she does. They listen defensively where Islam and some political problems are concerned. They consider their culture is older and superior, and think they understand Westerners better than most Arabs. They can disagree in a charming manner.

Arab countries (in general)

Not very good listeners, as they normally wish to speak, guide and philosophize. General hubbub in an Arab house/office makes careful listening difficult. Arabs listen better individually than in groups. A less than charismatic speaker may find they talk while he/she does. They listen defensively where Islam and some political problems are concerned. Speakers should maintain strong eye contact, get close to them, flatter a bit and raise the voice to indicate sincerity. After a general presentation, many Arabs come to the speaker for extra, private information.

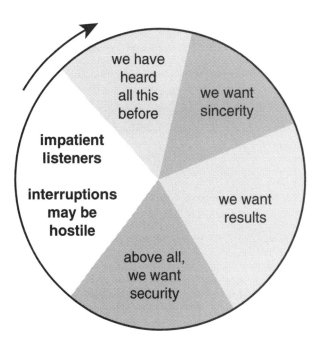

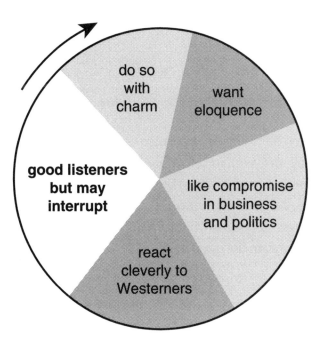

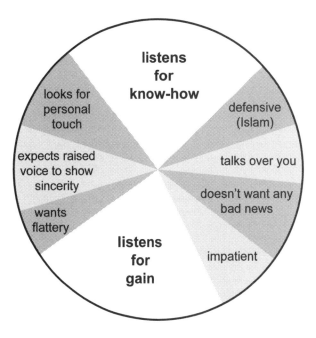

Central Asia
Azerbaijan, Kazakhstan, Uzbekistan, Kyrgyzstan, Tajikistan, Turkmenistan

Central Asians are careful listeners, as they wish to fasten on to any details which will give them benefits. They like to hear clear proposals, delivered forcefully and with energy. Leaders should be addressed directly, albeit courteously. Speakers should avoid contradicting opinions they know their audience holds. Criticisms must always be indirect and gentle. Muslim defensiveness can be high, but varies according to the country. Uzbeks are less patient listeners than the other peoples.

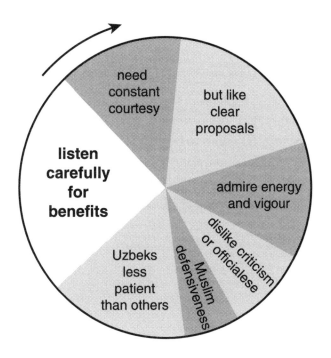

India

The key to Indian attention is to be eloquent, humble and respectful. They like flowery speech and an extensive vocabulary. They are willing to listen at length, to enable a relationship to develop and their aim, in the subsequent feedback, is to make a friend of the speaker. They are not difficult audiences, but their sagacity must not be underestimated.

Pakistan

Pakistanis' listening habits are similar to those of Indians, apart from Islamic defensiveness. The key to Pakistani attention is to be eloquent and respectful. They like vigorous speech and colourful vocabulary. They are willing to listen at length, to enable a relationship to develop and their aim, in the subsequent feedback, is to make an ally of the speaker. Their shrewdness must be taken into account.

Bangladesh

Bangladeshis listen carefully, as they have a thirst for knowledge. Their natural courtesy prevents them from interrupting frequently, though they may do so if they fail to understand what the speaker is driving at. As they listen, they are seeking areas of common interest and opportunities to create empathy. Sometimes they are reluctant to admit something is above their head, out of respect for a foreigner or senior figure. People from rural areas show more respect and understand less than urbanised Bangladeshis. Bangladeshis in general accept moralising and 'good advice' from well-educated people. They are, however, very sensitive and must not be talked down to. One must remember that their own education and cultural knowledge may be considerable. One should ask for their opinions, rather than just lecture them.

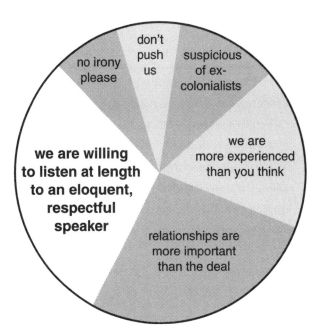

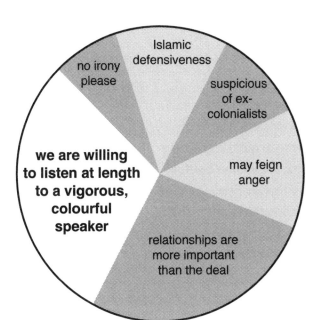

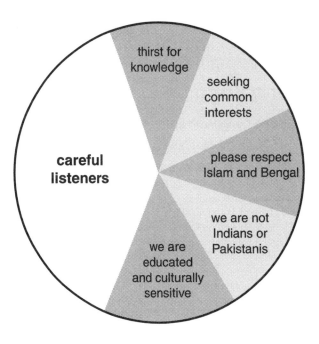

Japan

They pay careful attention to what is being said, and will listen with patience and in silence, as it is not usual to interrupt or ask questions until the end. Although difficulties with the language or unfamiliar train of thought may mean that not everything is understood, Japanese people will rarely ask for further explanations, as this might be considered impolite. Silence is not a negative sign in itself, as it usually means that the person is concentrating on what is being said, or reflecting on it. If eyes are closed during a meeting, this again shows that the person is listening intently.

China

Good listening is good manners in China. Being essentially reactive, they strive to accommodate the other side's wishes in their own proposals. Often reply with "My immature opinion is ..." Mainland Chinese are eager to acquire know-how from Westerners and Western markets for their products. They listen carefully and patiently in these areas, though most audiences are heavily dependent on interpreters. The manner of the speaker is considered more important than the content, so one needs to inject sufficient flattery and protect everyone's face. They are traditionally suspicious of "foreign devils", so work hard at creating trust.

Hong Kong

Hong Kong, with entrepreneurism in its blood, has a sense of urgency and always drives in the fast lane, standing in close comparison to the bustling USA. They listen for indications of factuality, competence, speed and bottom line.

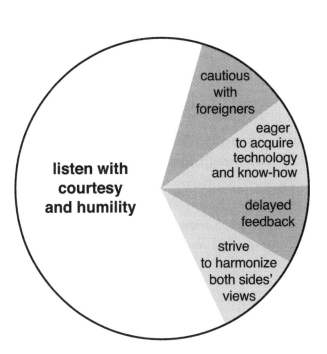

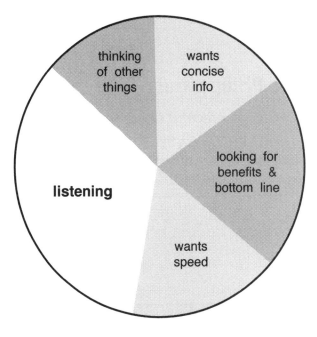

South Korea

Courteous listeners in true Asian style, but often giving the impression that they know in advance what you are going to tell them. The level of understanding is better than in Japan. Protection of face (kibun) is also of paramount importance among Koreans, who traditionally dislike foreigners, but disguise it well. Audiences are respectful, but Koreans like to show that they handle Westerners well and they often give lively feedback and ask original questions. They even like Western humour (which they profess to understand) so the odd joke or two might be attempted to soften them up.

North Korea

North Koreans make a difficult audience. Their cultural "black hole" is that all foreigners exploit Koreans and consequently Koreans hate all foreigners. They are particularly anti-American, but are hostile listeners even with South Koreans. Suspicion is their hallmark and attempts to win them over often founder on rocks of scepticism. Humour or levity is pointless – both are regarded as trickery. Only facts and figures count with them and even they are ruthlessly questioned. Go well prepared!

The Philippines

Although somewhat excitable and scattered in thought, Filipinos' Asian side makes them good, polite listeners. They like warm but modest speakers. Their comprehension of English is excellent and they give good, fluent feedback.

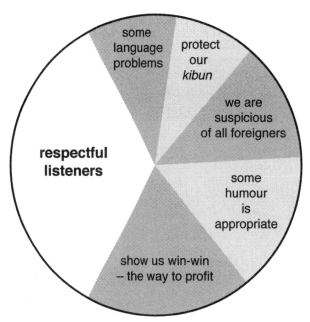

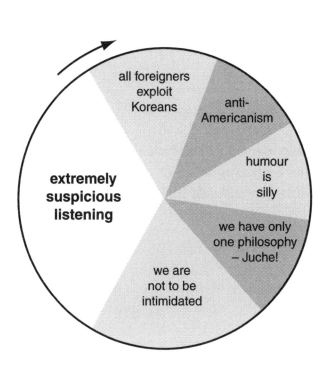

Thailand

Thais are docile, obedient listeners, who do not question a teacher's teaching. They give little feedback unless it is strongly requested. Sensitive discussion must be initiated from the top. They are fond of frequent, humorous interludes.

Vietnam

The Vietnamese are good listeners, expecting speakers to be clear and logical. They are well versed in French-style debate. They prefer presentations in French, but are becoming used to hearing English versions. They are hungry for advice and guidance as they reorganise their country, but feel they are culturally superior to many, and must not be talked down to.

Myanmar

Used to being harangued by the military and subjected to incessant propaganda, the Burmese listener adopts habitual passivity and hides powerful currents of scepticism. Devout Buddhists, who regularly practise meditation, Burmese take refuge in the ample solace offered by their religion and thousands take advantage of the education given by the numerous monasteries, which have no political axe to grind.

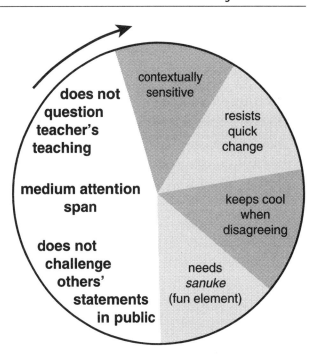

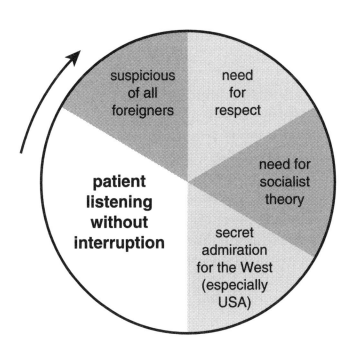

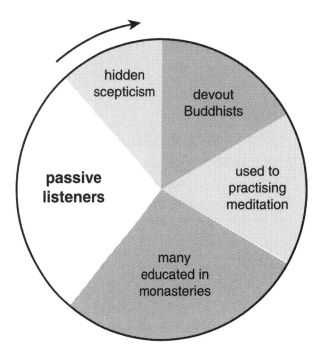

Singapore

Good listening is good manners in Singapore. Being essentially reactive, they strive to accommodate the other side's wishes in their own proposals. Often reply with "My immature opinion is…" Singaporeans are eager to acquire know-how from Westerners and Western markets for their products. They listen carefully and patiently in these areas. The manner of the speaker is considered more important than the content, so one needs to inject sufficient flattery and protect everyone's face.

Indonesia

They listen deferentially and do not interrupt. Speeches at public meetings are long and boring, but people show no dissension. In business meetings they listen carefully to foreigners, but do not always fully understand the content. Unfortunately they do not indicate this. Misunderstandings may arise. Indonesians, like Malaysians and other S.E. Asian people, are respectful listeners. Unlike Malaysians, they are often deficient in language skills and need careful repetition of all key points. Their questioning can be very simple, almost childlike; they rarely say anything to offend. Consequently it is often difficult to judge the relative success of one's presentation.

Malaysia

Listening is respectful and interruptions are few. People show no dissension, but Islamic defensiveness is increasing. In business meetings they listen carefully to foreigners. Misunderstandings may arise, but British English is more popular than American. The level of English is much higher than in Indonesia or Thailand.

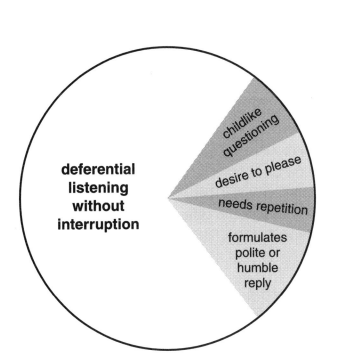

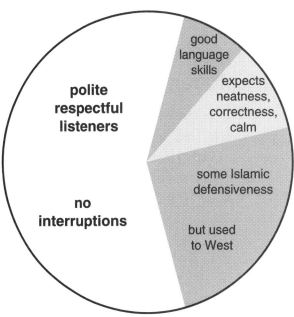

French North Africa

Formerly French-ruled North Africans – of Arab or Berber origin, but considerably westernised – are used to listening to lengthy French-style perorations which examine all aspects of an issue but seek a logical conclusion. Like the French, North Africans listen with respect, but feel they can interrupt if they disagree with the speaker or if they think the dialogue is going "off track". They respect statistics, but prefer to hear opinions. Being often rather pro-Western, they seek guidance and advice. They enjoy eloquence and are grateful for compassion or at least shows of understanding. They can become impatient if a presentation restricts itself largely to facts and figures.

Portuguese Africa

Angolan and Mozambican businesspeople are rather sophisticated listeners who expect logical argument, respect and occasionally compassion. With the rich resources they possess (especially Angola) they know they cannot be talked down to, and evince scepticism if a speaker departs from rationality. They like serious proposals (perhaps laced with humour) and look for solutions rather than problems. They may interrupt, but generally wait till the end, to give full feedback.

Sub-Saharan Africa

Africans are courteous listeners who drink in information, though some repetition is advisable. They do not like being rushed verbally – their own elders have innate patience putting forward concepts and discussing problems from all angles. Though suspicious of "ex-colonialists", Africans are quickly gratified by reasonable establishment of trust between parties.

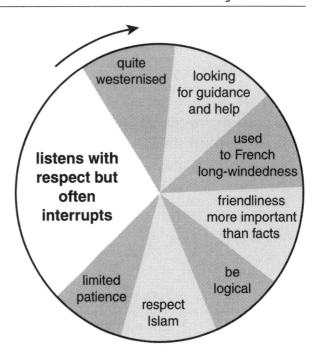

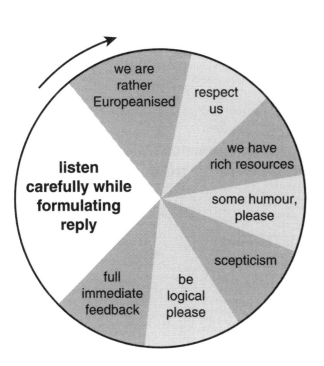

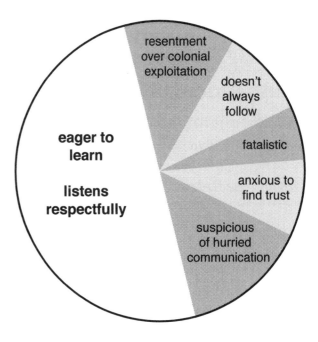

South Africa (black)

They are courteous listeners who are used to being talked to by their white compatriots. They do not like being rushed verbally – their own elders have innate patience. Though suspicious of white South Africans, blacks are quickly gratified by reasonable establishment of trust between parties. While scepticism is not rare, they appreciate that they are still on a learning curve and consequently like a well-thought-out and compassionate address.

South Africa (white British)

British South Africans are good, patient listeners and benefit from their multicultural experience. They are skilful at reading between the lines and do not impose their views quickly on non-whites. Manners are important, as is clear diction. Humour is always welcome.

South Africa (white Dutch)

Afrikaners, though often somewhat impatient, are good listeners on account of their multicultural experience. They are skilful at reading between the lines and do not impose their views quickly on non-whites, though they are less tactful than British South Africans. Afrikaners interrupt more than the British.

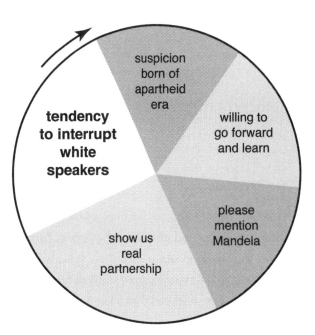

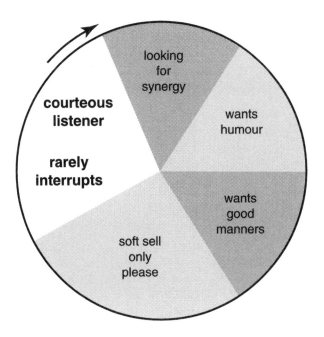

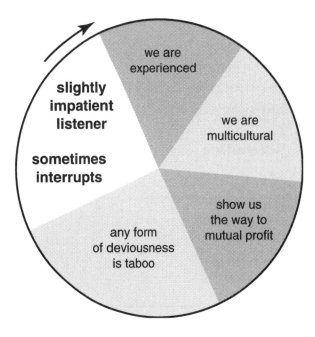

Australia

It is fatal to talk posh or be in any way pompous in front of Australians, who have a healthy and enduring disrespect for people in superior positions or those who seek to promote themselves. It is also inadvisable to be too serious or complicated. Australians are fond of jokes and anecdotes, preferably delivered in broad speech. A friendly and lively audience once they have decided to like you.

New Zealand

New Zealanders make excellent audiences inasmuch as they rarely interrupt and listen with care. They are, however, practised debaters and can be expected to provide immediate and pertinent feedback. Essentially democratic and tolerant, they nevertheless harbour a certain degree of scepticism, especially when listening to Australians, whom they regard as often brash, or Americans, whom they find hyperbolic and frequently slick. British and South African speakers generally hit the right note with New Zealand audiences.

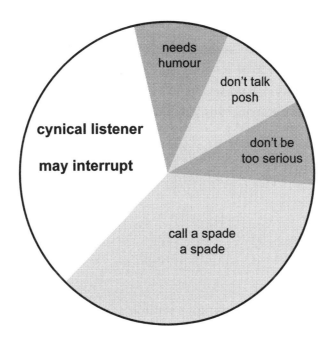

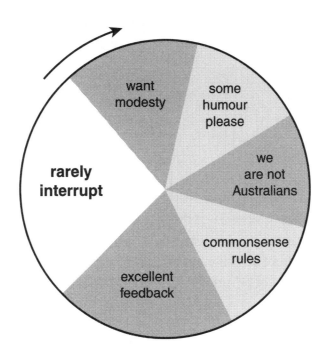

USA

Americans are active listeners and respond verbally and non-verbally to show their interest or lack of it. Generally, Americans listen closely to technical information and humorous anecdotes. They like to be entertained. As an audience, they expect the speaker to be convincing, hard-selling, to the point, persuasive and charismatic. If the speaker lacks these qualities, Americans get bored quickly. Their attention span is often short.

Canada

Canadians are polite listeners and rarely interrupt a sensible speech or presentation. It is, however, a basic tenet of Canadian education that even young people may challenge the precepts of others. Canadians excel in courteous give-and-take debate. Instruction in schools is less teacher-led than student-directed. Canadians like modest, unpretentious speakers who provide facts without trimmings and inject gentle humour into the process. Unlike Americans, they do not want the hard sell. They enjoy early debate with you, but listen politely to all you have to say first.

Mexico

Mexicans are warm-hearted people who make willing and pleasant audiences, provided they believe the speaker is sincere and they are getting a fair deal. This has not always been the case in the past with Anglo-Saxons. Material and personal honour are at the forefront of their minds as they hear someone out. They need time to reflect and will not be rushed into anything. They are very responsive to fairness and kindness.

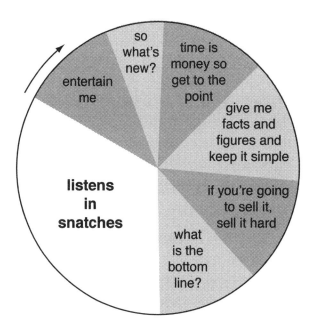

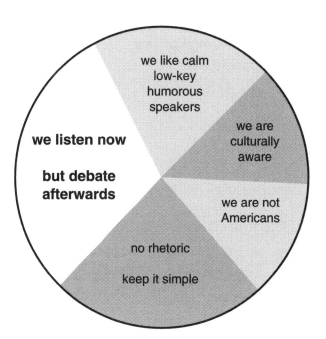

Hispanic America (in general)

Most Hispanic Americans are loquacious Latins who have been exploited sometime in the past by Americans or Europeans. Traditionally they are poor at co-operating with authorities or any external plans which do not correspond to their immediate needs. Consequently they are not among the best of audiences. Only charismatic speakers can get them to listen long, and even they must be very respectful and present the listeners with an intrinsic learning opportunity.

Brazil

Owing to the exuberance of expression of the Brazilians, their listening habits tend to be somewhat erratic – interrupting their interlocutor with ideas of their own, each individual wanting to make his or her personal contribution. They aim to form an in-depth impression of the speaker from watching his movements, gestures and eye contact, rather than listening intently to what is being said. They have a relatively short attention span. Among South Americans, Brazilians are perhaps the most receptive to foreign ideas, perhaps because their break with their colonial masters – Portugal – was amicable. The key to their attention is to talk enough about Brazil (even Brazilian football) and be invariably cheerful bordering on euphoric. They are not really recording efficiently what you actually say, but eagerly seeking "simpatismo" to enable them to do business with someone they like.

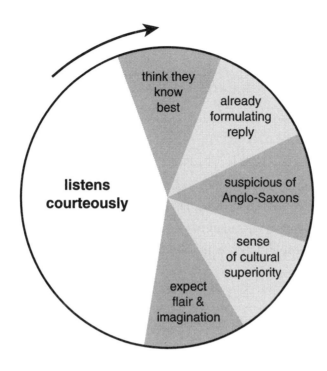

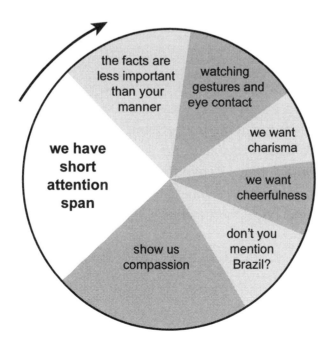

Cuba

In view of their relative isolation from many parts of the world, Cubans are eager listeners, hungry for knowledge and know-how. Their high level of general education enables them to put new information into perspective, but anti-Americanism lurks in the background as a result of government influence.

Jamaica

Jamaicans are masters of the art of listening and talking at the same time. Meetings are very interactive, as are radio shows where callers and moderators take rapid turns. This phenomenon is part of the social fabric of the country. When speakers outline benefits for Jamaicans, they are suddenly attentive and quiet. If things are not developing well, disapproval is voiced in the form of interruptions or chatting amongst themselves. This often is done humorously and the audience also expects a modicum of humour from the speaker.

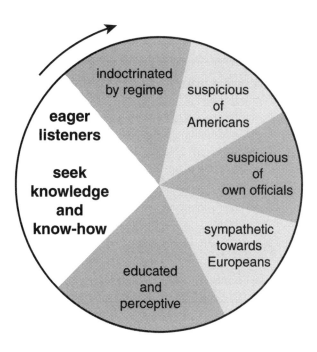

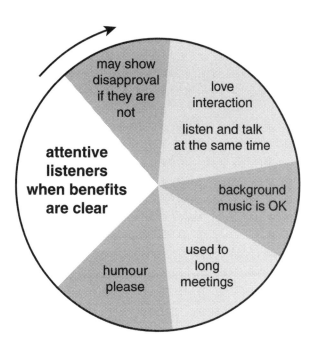

Exercises

1 **In what way do you listen? Describe your listening habits briefly in words below:**

-
-
-
-
-
-
-

2 **Now draw a diagram to describe your own listening habits in the space below, combining words and visuals:**

3 **Flick through the listening habit diagrams on pages 61-113. Which cultures are you most similar to and which ones do you differ from? Write them down below:**

Similar   *Different*

·   ·

·   ·

·   ·

·   ·

·   ·

4 **Now draw two diagrams below (combining words and visuals) for a colleague you find easy to listen to, and a colleague you find hard to listen to:**

Easy listening   *Hard listening*

Audience Expectations during Presentations

In an era of galloping globalisation of trade, political intercourse and social interaction, there is an increasing need for people of different nationalities and cultures to reach out to each other to facilitate mutual understanding.

Company executives, salespeople, politicians, international social workers, peace-keepers, academics and scientists are all obliged to present their cases – be they strategies, opinions, directives or simply wares and products – to a large number of audiences of distinctly varying cultural backgrounds and world views. These audiences – whether they attend a presentation to seek profit, aid, instruction or clarification of the details of a merger or joint venture – bring with them a set of expectations as to the content, style and purpose of the address. These expectations are born of past experience of such events, usually in their own country and delivered by their own compatriots. Their own countrymen are familiar with local or national listening habits and automatically cater to these, or other expectations, often with consummate skill.

Thousands of presentations are given daily, around the world, increasingly in an international ambience, usually (but not always) in the English language. If speakers/ presenters do not meet the expectations of the audience before them, whether they seek profit, obedience or simply compliance, they will be less than successful in their aims and will miss out on a great opportunity (having succeeded in getting the audience together in the first place). It is advisable, even essential, to know why the audience actually turned up. What do they want to hear?

Expectations vary wildly. Americans come to a presentation to be entertained, at least initially. They do not like being bored. Germans do not mind being bored as long as they are fed real information. Finns expect a speaker to say only what is absolutely necessary with a minimum of words and no rhetoric. Italians, on the other hand, expect rhetoric, charisma and elegant persuasion from a well-dressed speaker. Spaniards, too, expect warmth and friendliness and thrive on strong eye contact. Swedes, like Germans, are used to long explanatory consensus-seeking meetings with an abundance of contextual details and clear structure – beginning, middle and ending. First you tell them what you are going to tell them, then you tell them, then you tell them what you have told them. Such an approach would drive a French person mad ("Je ne suis pas stupide"). French expect early wit, originality and innovative ideas, otherwise you quickly lose them. Japanese, on the other hand, could not care less what you say as long as you say it nicely and courteously, and wear a dark suit. They come to a first presentation, often in large numbers, not to understand but to show solidarity and seek harmony. Chinese expect humility above all, Indians flowery Victorian speech; Africans warmth and repetition; Arabs shouting to show sincerity.

Different areas and cultural groupings display some commonalities in audience expectations. The British need for persistent humour is shared to a large extent by Americans, Canadians, Australians and New Zealanders. Scandinavians come closest to the Anglo-Saxons in their concept of and preference for humour; Norwegians and Danes want it spiced with mild cynicism. British want their humour subtle; Australians like it cheeky and often irreverent. Germans, Japanese and Chinese can manage without it.

East of Istanbul, and especially in Asia, face protection is essential and Western speakers should keep this at the forefront of their presentation. Malaysians and Vietnamese like well-structured addresses, with British and French models respectively in mind. Indonesians are used to long, boring perorations. Thais, on the other hand, want a bit of fun thrown in. Among Asian audiences, Filipinos are closest to Westerners; profit-minded Koreans try to be, but are inherently suspicious. In Russia and former communist-ruled countries in Eastern Europe, a personal style of address will pay dividends. Previously anything official portended a lie, whereas strong personal opinions, even rumours, heralded the truth.

England	Scotland
• humour • a story • "nice" product • reasonable price • quality • traditional rather than modern • understatement • low key presentation • no hard sell	• humour • reference to Scotland • facts • hard-headedness • some romanticism • mild rhetoric • way to profit • warmth • thrift

Ireland	Wales
• humour (some irony allowed) • charm • facts (some embellishment permitted) • informality, friendliness • poetic or romantic touch • background of culture • tolerance • interesting, lively presentation • some folksiness • simplicity of approach towards reasonable solutions	• a humorous opening • folksy style • plain facts • no hard sell • sincerity • recognition of their Welshness

Germany	Italy	France
• solidity of company • solidity of product • technical info • context • beginning – middle – ending • lots of print • few or no jokes • soft sell • good price • quality • delivery date	• friendliness • flexibility • style • tasteful product • elegance • well-dressed • personality • laughter • some cultural reference • delicacy • design-conscious	• formality • innovative product • "sexy" appeal • imagination • logical presentation • reference to France • style, appearance • personal touch • a little irony • may interrupt

Switzerland	Spain	The Netherlands
• calm and courteous listeners • expect formality • want logic • pragmatic • looking for solidity • humour accepted but not necessary • price conscious • concerned about quality • precise about delivery dates • no hard sell • no bombast • well-dressed presenters • technical facts	• warmth • originality • eloquence • liveliness • strong eye contact • humour • overt body language • charisma • good price • personal touch	• recognition of Dutch internationalism and incredible economic achievements • interesting product • facts, facts, facts • no sarcasm, only few jokes • lots of print • no extravagance • no time-wasting • open discussion • no hard sell • show way to mutual profit • well-prepared, well-informed speaker • competence

Austria (Vienna)	Austria (Tirol)	Portugal
• expect sophistication • wary of being cornered • ready for compromise • polite and agreeable all round • anxious to speak soon • avoid confrontation • expect speaker to be well-dressed • like conservatism • formality	• factuality • conservatism • no rhetoric • neatness • "Ordnung" • some rusticity • common sense • well-dressed speaker • punctuality • structured presentation	• sophisticated discourse • human understanding • compassion • some rhetoric, liveliness • some restraint • knowledge of Portuguese history • we are not Spaniards • international outlook • extreme friendliness

Belgium (Flemish)	Belgium (Walloon)	Greece
• we want facts • we cooperate • we are not Walloons • we are not Dutch • we like humility • we dislike rhetoric and charisma • tell us the strategy • no bombast • quality counts	• facts and some feelings • we cooperate • we are not Flemish • we are not French • we like humility • no rhetoric but a little charisma is OK • give us instructions • no bombast • quality counts	• eloquence • sophistication • pragmatism and experience • well-dressed speaker • compassion and human understanding • historical perspective • aesthetic sense • flexibility • knowledge of Greek history • charisma • show us the way to profit

Finland	Sweden
• modernity • quality • technical info • modest presentation • design • few words • no flattery (males) • soft sell • no impositions • we are not Swedes	• modernity • quality • design • technical info • delivery dates • no rhetoric • smoothness • mutual acceptance • consideration • respect Welfare State
Denmark	**Norway**
• best design • quality • delivery date • modernity • quiet, rational presentation • humour • technical info • no bombast • keep it cosy • no assertiveness	• egalitarian approach • brisk style • quiet confidence in product • no overstating • clean design • quality product • technical information • solidity • Norway is best

Estonia	Latvia	Lithuania
<ul><li>goals and logic must be explicit</li><li>presentations must have clear structure</li><li>speaker must show education</li><li>no long-windedness</li><li>no time-wasting</li><li>good preparation appreciated</li><li>modernity</li><li>innovative product</li></ul>	<ul><li>good structure and planning</li><li>a cool approach</li><li>some modesty and reticence</li><li>escape from (Soviet) "officialese"</li><li>reference to EU orientation</li><li>education and sophistication</li><li>modernity</li><li>soft sell</li><li>no hurry</li></ul>	<ul><li>erudition and knowledge</li><li>facts and figures combined with warmth</li><li>eloquence and spontaneity</li><li>recognition of Lithuania's past</li><li>dislike of officialdom</li><li>eagerness for Western contact</li><li>wish to debate</li></ul>

Poland	Hungary	The Czech Republic
<ul><li>recognition</li><li>logic</li><li>sentiment</li><li>distrust officials</li><li>personal touch</li><li>no pressure or brute force</li><li>concessions</li><li>favourable deal</li><li>romanticism</li><li>love of Poland</li></ul>	<ul><li>theatricality</li><li>verbosity</li><li>humour</li><li>feelings</li><li>charm</li><li>context</li><li>respect</li><li>artistry</li><li>sophistication</li><li>good deal</li><li>shrewdness</li><li>nimbleness</li></ul>	<ul><li>need facts and figures</li><li>want calm speaker</li><li>logic important</li><li>low key – nothing flamboyant</li><li>want recognition of Czech sophistication</li><li>welcome innovation</li><li>want solutions rather than problems</li><li>humour necessary (some black humour is acceptable)</li><li>we are not Slovaks</li></ul>

Slovakia	Bulgaria	Romania
• information please • plenty of context • some charisma • instructions, especially in Western business methods • warmth and generosity • sophistication of discourse • recognition of Slovakia • soft sell • we are not Czechs	• high level of education • know-how • integrity and reserve • new (modern) ideas • advice and encouragement • roundabout discussion • well-dressed speakers • pragmatic conclusions • the next step • win-win exit	• reference to their uniqueness • sophistication of discourse • logical arguments • personal style of delivery • some charisma, even hyperbole • flexible truth • well-dressed speakers • delicacy and indirectness • no talking down to them • no ideology (any more)
Serbia & Montenegro	Slovenia	Croatia
• sympathy for Serb cause • help in difficulties • opinions to be expressed clearly • word-deed correlation • some charisma • liveliness and rhetoric • interruptions acceptable • audience will want to speak soon • wary of being cornered	• need clear information • no emotive content, please • plenty of context required • low key discourse • well-dressed presenters • recognition of Slovenian achievements • we are not Serbs (or even Croats) • please be logical • make words count	• want logical arguments spiced with a little verve • are suspicious of rhetoric or too much charisma • they "lean West" • speakers should be well-dressed • like reference to "new Croatia" • appreciate humour • don't confuse us with Serbs • expect sophistication • are fairly international • warm to a speaker slowly (not before trust has been established)

Russia	Ukraine	Belarus
• official view is a lie • personal view is true • changes are always bad • suspicious of foreigners • expects rhetoric • expects sentiment • expects complexity • needs recognition • people-oriented • conspiratorial • no war talk • dislikes greed • let's beat the system	• do you lean East or West? • make your own case • emotional speech • considerable body language • respect Ukraine's independence • what can you offer us? • sincerity, please • spice it with humour • we like anecdotes and examples • don't pull wool over our eyes • we are not Russians and have a long separate history • remember we live next to Russia	• hearing woes • keeping quiet • share emotions of speaker • voicing own opinions may be a nuisance • open debate unlikely • show us profit NOW • "a bird in the hand..." • distrust of officialdom • we have heard this before...

Turkey	Iran	Israel
• warmth • controlled rhetoric • understanding • want some solidarity with West • like some mention of Turkey • willing to learn • don't interrupt • give slow feedback • looking for trust	• respect for the Revolution • that aside, pragmatism • formal, ultra polite opening • then get to the point without delay • share your know-how with us • no strings, please • match our intellectual level • match our cultural level • remember we are not Arabs • know our glorious past • invest in our great future potential	• honesty, sincerity and directness • some help • facts, figures and pragmatism • life is hard – let's face it • some defence of Israeli actions • some practical solutions • educated approach • experience

Iraq	Egypt	Arab countries
• sincerity please • we have heard this before... • impartiality • compassion • please offer solutions • we respect education • warmth • look us in the eye • firm hand is OK • security (above all)	• reference to Egypt's glorious history • education and sophistication • warmth • liveliness (but with some restraint) • cosmopolitanism • personal touch • international outlook • familiarity with Westerners • combines faith with pragmatism • tolerance • patience	• rhetoric • eloquence • liveliness • personal touch • clean appearance • education • know-how • respect • physical proximity • strong eye contact • Allah is great • wants "extra talk" afterwards
India	**Pakistan**	**Bangladesh**
• humility • flowery speech • respect • know-how • trust • flexibility • tolerance for ambiguity • sympathy • patience / rock bottom prices • acknowledgement of India's potential	• fairness • eloquent speech • respect Islam • know-how • flexibility • tolerance for ambiguity • patience / rock bottom prices • we are no longer Indians • know our history	• speaker should be knowledgeable • humility • eloquence • tolerance of diverse views and beliefs • understanding • empathy towards Bangladeshis and their difficulties (poverty, flooding) • we are not Indians or Pakistanis • awareness of the internal diversity inside Bangladesh • respect for Islam • respect for Bengal

Kazakhstan	Uzbekistan	Turkmenistan
• admire energy and vigour • want clear proposals • expect constant courtesy • slight Muslim defensiveness • dislike criticism • avoid losing face • getting used to Westerners • pragmatism • want praise for Kazakhstan	• impatient listeners • want to speak themselves • want to know bottom line • have good opinion of themselves • crafty in extracting benefits • suspicious of "officialese" • perceptive • used to doing deals • spiritual values important	• suspicious of foreigners • nationalistic • want respect for their peculiar social customs • expect courtesy • want pragmatism • gas is their strong card • anti-Russian • males dominate
Azerbaijan	Kyrgyzstan	Tajikistan
• play their oil-rich card • remember they are anti-Armenian, but pro-Turkish • used to dealing with West • opportunistic • expect good deals • moderate Islamic defensiveness • keen on investment • anti-Russian	• pro-Turkish, anti-Russian • democratically inclined • rural attitudes • eager for sincerity • seek trust • prefer Kazakhs to Uzbeks • dislike hurried pace • dignity-conscious • consider proposals cautiously	• Indo-European language • gives them kinship with Iranians • anti-Uzbek • patient listeners • religion important • need extreme politeness • relaxed attitude to time • expect help • open to suggestions • some passivity

Japan	China	Hong Kong
• good price • USP (unique selling point) • synergy with company image • harmony • politeness • respect for their Company • good name of your Company • quiet presentation • well-dressed presenter • formality • diagrams • modesty	• know-how • humble tone • reserve and patience • investment from you • long term view • licensing • help and advice • equality of treatment • older speakers preferred • respect for their elders • China is the centre of the world	• competence • humble tone • speed • licensing • pragmatic suggestions • older speakers • show us the way to profit • technological short cuts • innovation • no red tape • we are not mainlanders
South Korea	**North Korea**	**The Philippines**
• respect • reserve • hard facts • clear English • well-dressed • need trust • win-win prospect • the way to profit • quick solutions • some humour	• recognition of Juche • mention leader • accept our views • no brainwashing • this meeting is at your request • show us what you can give us • speak clearly • dress well • distrust of foreigners in general	• jealous of freedom of speech • may interrupt politely • suspicious of officialdom • normally fluent in English • want warmth and understanding • look for modesty • want their face protected • body language is important • speakers must be neat and clean • like to be instructed • sense of humour • wish to develop relationships

Thailand	Vietnam	Myanmar
• listen for know-how • expect gentleness and courtesy • want clear guidelines • respect shown to superiors • message must be fun-oriented • unhurried pace • humour welcomed • patience expected • need friendliness	• logical argument • elegant structure • modern presentation • some feeling (French influence) • some praise for Vietnamese heroism • socialist orthodoxy (currently) • entrepreneurial ideas (especially in the South) • culture • respect for tradition • debating skill	• please minimise the propaganda • show your devoutness • respect Theravada Buddhism • good speakers are gentle and non-assertive • we may have to hide our reactions to you ("walls have ears") • refer to the beauty of our country and architecture • be patient with our current difficulties (we may be a future Tiger)
Singapore	**Indonesia**	**Malaysia**
• know-how • humble tone • reserve and patience • export prospects • long-term view • licensing • equality of treatment • older speakers • respect for their elders • acknowledgement of Singapore's achievements • respect both democracy and hierarchy	• courtesy and gentleness • friendliness • relations more important than profits • quiet presentation • neat appearance • no hurry • focus on Indonesia's achievements rather than shortcomings • everything is negotiable	• politeness and gentleness • education • relations more important than profits • modest presentation • clean appearance • no haste • focus on Malaysia's achievements rather than shortcomings • everything is negotiable • we are multi-racial • we are increasingly Islamic

French North Africa	Portuguese Africa	Sub-Saharan Africa
• good French • English common medium • logic • controlled rhetoric • knowledge of their history (including Berber) • sophistication • know-how • good eye contact • clear articulation • lengthy delivery • understanding of their problems	• sophistication • compassion • knowledge of Portuguese African history • partnership for gain • some humour or wit • friendly "we-are-equals" tone • clear speech • imagination • ultimate pragmatism • recognition of our size and potential	• warmth • friendliness • humanity • sincerity • trust • no patronising • no hurry • some humour • no "jungle" words • professional appearance • concessions • physical proximity • help us
South Africa (black)	**South Africa** (white British)	**South Africa** (white Dutch)
• recognition of New South Africa • mention of Mandela • sincerity • trust • no patronising • no haste • some humour • professional appearance • concessions • physical proximity • warmth and friendliness • partnership	• facts • accuracy • understanding of African conditions • professional appearance • humour • business-like attitude • entrepreneurial stance • sense of adventure • realism • irony OK	• facts and figures • neatness • understanding of African conditions • professional appearance • hearty humour • business-like attitude • entrepreneurial stance • sense of adventure • realism • acknowledge Dutch / Afrikaner contribution

Australia	New Zealand	
• matey opening • informality throughout • humour • persuasive style • no padding • little contexting • call a spade a spade • innovative product • essential technical info • personal touch • may interrupt • imaginative conclusion	• conservatism • common sense • low key • no flattery (males) • show way to profit • recognition of small-but-good concept • we are not Australians • we are good at business (especially when we emigrate)	
USA	**Canada**	**Mexico**
• humorous opening • joking maintained • generosity • modernity • gimmicks • slogans • catch phrases • hard sell • speed • USA is best	• low key presentation • technical facts • no ostentation • no hard sell • plenty of context • tolerance • humour • quick feedback and debate • cultural sensitivity • we are not Americans	• national honour must be satisfied • eloquence and rhetoric expected • lengthy discourse • compassion important • suspicious of Americans • want warmth • looking for business • crave idealism over materialism • don't want to be rushed • relationship more important than product

Hispanic America	Brazil
• expect exploitation • expect arrogance • suspicious listeners • conceal suspicion with politeness • want adventurous ideas • want friendliness • expect overt body language • need strong eye contact • need compassion • we are cultured • we were not born yesterday	• extreme friendliness • compassion • mention Brazil • cheerfulness • mention football • informality • optimism • relationship before product • theatricality • exuberance • loquacity
Cuba	Jamaica
• extreme friendliness • compassion and understanding of their difficulties • music, music • racial tolerance • cheerfulness • humanity • like to visit Europe • cautious about USA • proud of Cuba's achievements in health and education • mention sport	• warmth and humour • possibility to interact • content supersedes everything else • length is OK • presenter must have speaking skills • presenter must be animated • background music helps • laid-back style is OK, but arguments must be authentic and convincing • feasible scenarios • long term and tangible results sought

Exercises

1 | When participating in an audience, what are your own expectations with regard to the speaker? Please describe in words below:

-
-
-
-
-
-

2 | What do you think are the typical audience expectations of a **"Linear-active"** culture? Describe below in words:

(see page 274 for a description of Linear-active)

-
-
-
-
-
-
-
-
-
-
-

3 | What do you think are the typical audience expectations of a **"Multi-active"** culture? Describe below in words:

(see page 274 for a description of Multi-active)

-
-
-
-
-
-
-
-
-
-
-

4 What do you think are the typical audience expectations of a **"Reactive"** culture?
Describe below in words: (see pages 274-275 for a description of Reactive)

-
-
-
-
-
-

-
-
-
-
-
-

5 Consider presentations you have made in the past to audiences not of your own nationality. Which nationalities were easy to present to, which were difficult?

Easy presentation

-
-
-
-
-

Difficult presentation

-
-
-
-
-

6 Will you be making a presentation soon to an audience comprising other cultures? Visit **www.crossculture.com/visualapproach**, describe your situation, and we will offer you some advice.

7 At **www.cultureactive.com**, you can take a cultural assessment that will tell you which of the three categories – linear-active, multi-active or reactive – you personally belong to. You can then compare yourself to other cultures online.

Leadership Styles

Different cultures have diverse concepts of leadership. Leaders can be born, elected, or trained and groomed. Others seize power or have leadership thrust upon them. Leadership can be autocratic or democratic, collective or individual, meritocratic or unearned, desired or imposed.

It is not surprising that business leaders (managers) often wield their power in conformity with the national set-up – for instance a confirmed democracy like Sweden produces low key democratic managers; Arab managers are good Muslims; Chinese managers usually have government or Party affiliations.

Leaders cannot readily be transferred from culture to culture. Japanese Prime Ministers would be largely ineffective in the United States; American politicians would fare badly in most Arab countries; Mullahs would not be tolerated in Norway. Similarly, business managers find the transition from one culture to another fraught with difficulties. Such transfers become more and more common with the globalisation of business, but the composition of international teams and particularly the choice of their leaders, requires careful thought. Autocratic French managers have to tread warily in consensus-minded Japan or Sweden. Courteous Asian leaders would have to adopt a more vigorous style in argumentative Holland or theatrical Spain if they wished to hold the stage. German managers sent to Australia are somewhat alarmed at the irreverence of their staff and their apparent lack of respect for authority.

England

In some companies the managers, though not entirely autocratic, maintain considerable power distance between themselves and their staff. More common today, however, is the rather casual manager who sits just outside the ring of executives, but is in close contact with them and well able to conduct effective supervision without interfering unduly with the daily routine. British managers could be described as diplomatic, tactful, laid back, casual, reasonable, helpful, willing to compromise and seeking to be fair. They also consider themselves to be inventive and, on occasion, lateral thinkers. They see themselves as conducting business with grace, style, humour, wit, eloquence and self possession. They have the English fondness for debate and regard meetings as occasions to seek agreement rather than to issue instructions.

Scotland

Throughout history, Scots have remained fiercely loyal to their clan and these leanings, though less obvious in modern commercial enterprises, are often in the background. Apart from questions of clan hierarchy, power distance is low and leadership is very democratic. Many Scots seem to be "born leaders", inasmuch as they have figured conspicuously as inspirational personages in British politics and the Civil Service. Their leadership qualities have frequently been evidenced in the days of Empire, where Scots gained fame as explorers, generals and high-ranking administrators.

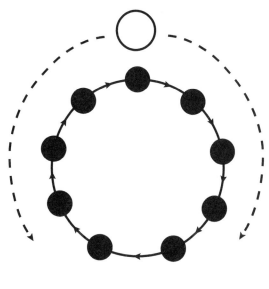

casual leadership

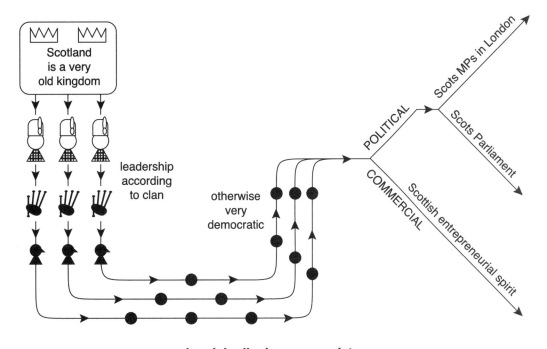

clannish allegiances persist

Ireland

The Church has exercised enormous influence over Irish life for many centuries. Leadership has tended to be autocratic and centralised in the Latin manner. Irish kings, Viking chieftains and ecclesiastical luminaries have all enjoyed considerable status vis-à-vis a rural and somewhat cowed populace. Since the establishment of democracy, Irish leaders have generally emerged as charismatic persons with an educated background. As politics are often stormy, those who get on with different factions and have the ability to persuade and arbitrate are most likely to rise to the top. Women are in the ascendancy.

Wales

The Welsh leadership style is not dissimilar to the Swedish, where managers and staff sit in a circle and try to reach consensus. Music, choirs and rugby are binding factors and the relative smallness of many Welsh enterprises removes possible elements of pomposity or excessive charisma. "Let's pull together" is the spirit – power distance is low.

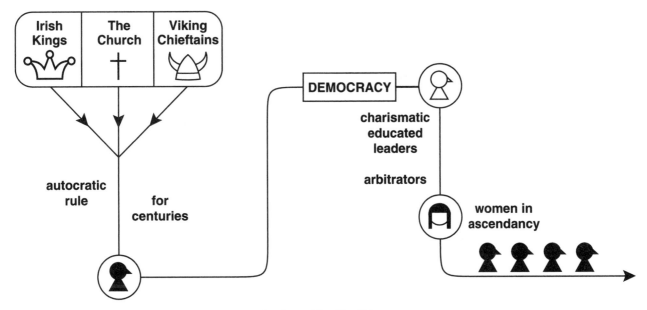

charismatic, flexible

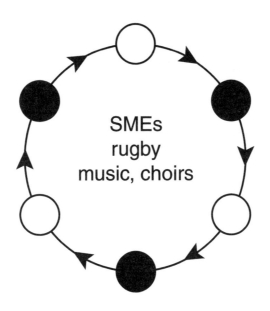

cosy circle leadership

Germany

The basic principle of German management is that you put the most experienced, best-educated person at the top and he/she instructs and guides meticulously his/her immediate subordinate. Orders are passed down through the management structure in this manner. Though leadership is consequently hierarchical and autocratic, German leaders do listen to suggestions "from the factory floor", as German workers are generally well-educated and inventive. In this way, consensus plays a part in German business. Hierarchy, however, generally dominates.

Italy

Italian leadership is basically autocratic, but shows more flexibility than some other Latin styles, as managers mingle easily with staff and intersperse themselves at many levels. There are many "clan" and group interests in the southern half of the country and loyalty to the leader is automatic and mandatory. In Milan, Turin and Genoa, there is a growing tendency to select managers on merit. In the north in general, professional competence is valued, though connections remain important. Basically, Italians are comfortable in a hierarchy skilfully led by persons of noble birth or from traditionally eminent or wealthy families. The patronage system is well established in the southern part of the country, especially in Sicily.

France

In France, authority is centred around the chief executive. Top managers, are well-trained, charismatic and extremely autocratic. They often appear to consult with middle managers, technical staff – even workers – but decisions are generally personal and orders are top-down. Managers at this élite level are rarely fired when they make blunders.

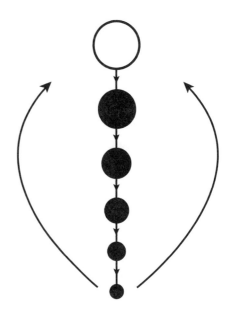

hierarchy + consensus

flexible autocracy

autocratic

Switzerland

As in the US, there is a deep-rooted distrust of government in Switzerland and the system of rule resembles the American in its intricate and delicate array of checks and balances. The President has some powers, but only one year to exercise them, and is closely bound by the Federal Council of Seven and the frequent referenda.

Spain

Spanish leaders, like French, are autocratic and charismatic. Unlike the French, they work less from logic than from intuition and pride themselves on their personal influence on all their staff members. Possessed often of great human force, they are able to persuade and inspire at all levels. Nepotism is also common in many companies. Declamatory in style, Spanish managers often see their decisions as irreversible.

The Netherlands

Leadership in the Netherlands is based on merit, competence and achievement. Managers are vigorous and decisive, but consensus is mandatory, as there are many key players in the decision making process. Long "Dutch debates" lead to action, taken at the top, but with constant reference to the "ranks". Ideas from low levels are allowed to filter freely upwards in the hierarchy.

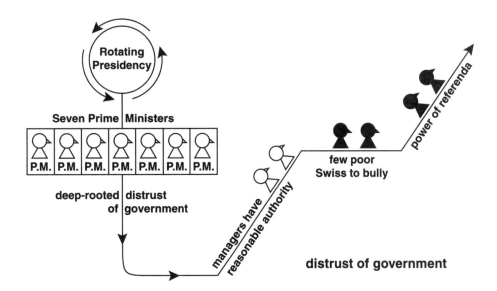

distrust of government

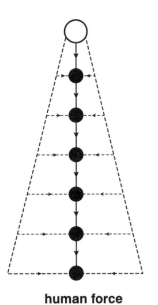

human force

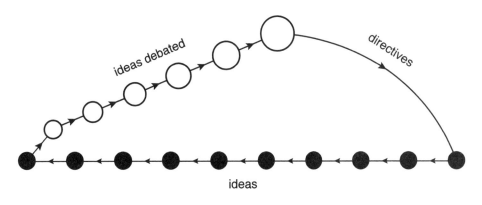

meritocratic, debating

Austria (Vienna)

At business level, leadership is autocratic and authoritarian. Staff listen respectfully to what the boss has got to say, without interrupting. Top managers maintain a sizeable power distance and delegate day-to-day tasks to middle managers, who work harder than they do. Middle managers enjoy authority over the rank and file, but object to the boss's policies at some risk. Workers tend to show exaggerated respect to seniors and are uncomfortable with a system where their voices are rarely heard and where the major societal decisions are made behind closed doors. The general lack of self-confidence (observable at all levels of Austrian society) discourages workers from standing up for their rights. Family connections and private networks are influential and advancement in business and government is less transparent than it seems. The younger generation feel they are inadequately represented. Many Austrians list "knowing the right people" as the most important factor in advancing one's career; hard work and loyalty to the company come lower down.

Austria (Tirol)

Leadership in western Austrian society is characterised by discipline and acceptance of authority. It is less formal than in Germany and less complex than in Vienna. Merit is important.

Portugal

Portugal is becoming a meritocracy, but still business leaders and many political figures come from the leading families. Portuguese senior executives make personal decisions, often in a family business context. Staff are generally obedient and deferential.

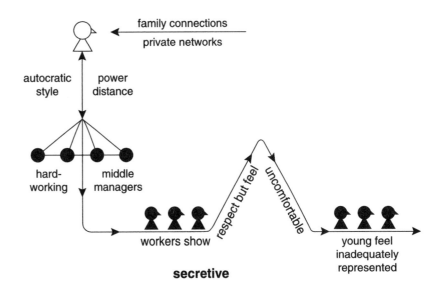

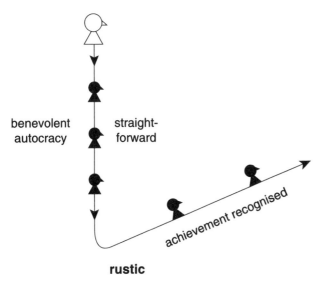

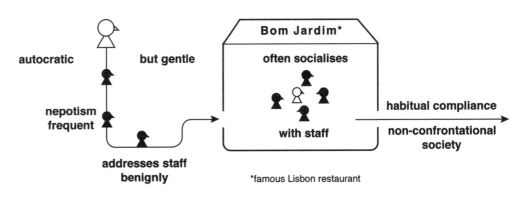

Belgium (Flemish)

Bosses are relaxed and low key and it is generally accepted that decision-making will be consensual. Responsibility is delegated downwards to a considerable degree. The similarity with Sweden is striking.

Belgium (Walloon)

Leadership is exercised in a manner close to the French, where all final decisions rest with the boss. There is normally a general airing of ideas among staff, but this is more a fact-finding exercise rather than a referendum-style discussion.

Greece

Military figures as well as patriarchs of the Eastern Orthodox Church exercised great influence in the political sphere in the 1960s and 1970s, but their power has declined in the past three decades. The King was quite popular in the post-war period, but the monarchy was abolished in 1973. In the world of business, management is autocratic.

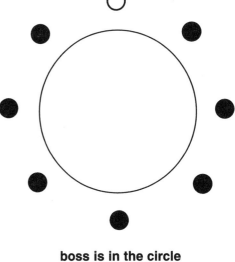

boss is in the circle

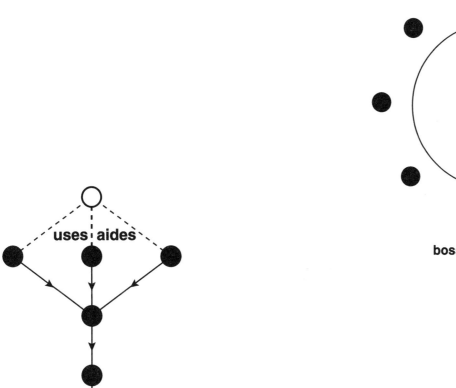

uses aides

autocratic and considerate

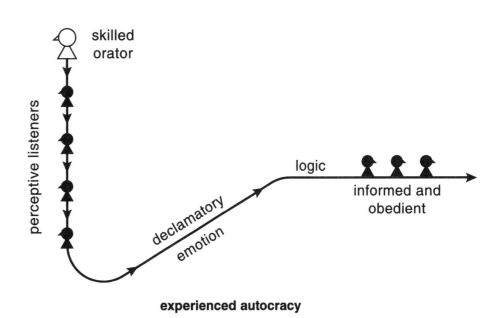

experienced autocracy

Finland

Finnish leaders, like many British, exercise control from a position just outside and above the ring of middle managers, who are allowed to make day-to-day decisions. Finnish top executives have the reputation of being decisive at crunch time and do not hesitate to stand shoulder to shoulder with staff and help out in crises. Finnish business history is short, but it is replete with a succession of self-made men and rugged individuals who created the companies which are household names in the country today. Such men are less in evidence as business-by-consensus comes into vogue, but their tradition lives on in Finnish respect for the strong leader who plunges onwards. Most Finnish managers make decisions without constant reference to HQ and this agility and mobile management is seen as a David-like advantage when dealing with foreign corporations of Goliathan proportions.

Sweden

Swedish managers are the least autocratic in the world and sit in the ring consulting with all at executive level and often with quite subordinate staff members. It is said Swedish managers wield power by appearing non-powerful. This style, ubiquitous in Sweden and popular with Swedes, is hardly conducive to rapid decision-making.

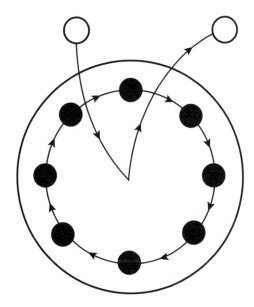

officer helps out in crisis

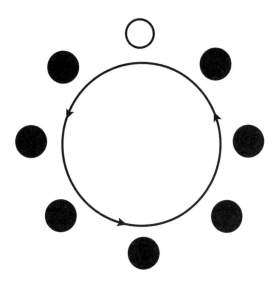

first among equals

Denmark

Danish top executives and middle managers are not always clearly distinguishable for non-Danes. Managers of all levels mingle for decision-making and democratic procedures are mandatory. Though top managers can exert considerable pressure, Danes are skilful in maintaining a decidedly congenial atmosphere in discussion. Horizontal communication is widespread and generally successful. Basic Danish assumptions are generally in line with their essentially democratic stance and Protestant fine tuning. Leadership is by achievement and demonstration of technical competence. Leaders are expected to be low profile, benign, consulting colleagues for opinions. Status is based on qualifications, competence and results, yet materialism is downplayed. There is a focus on welfare.

Norway

In democratic Norway, the boss is very much in the centre of things and staff enjoy access to him/her at most times. Middle managers' opinions are heard and acted upon in egalitarian fashion, but top executives rarely abandon responsibility and accountability.

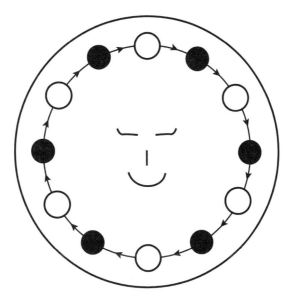

cosy, (*hygge*) all round

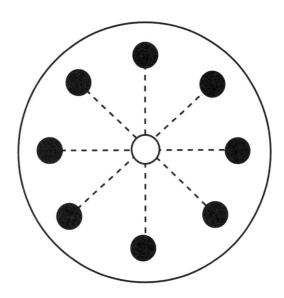

boss, but friendly

Estonia

Estonians are very individualistic. Everyone is a leader and no one likes being led. Estonia does not have a hierarchical system. It has never had its own aristocracy, only foreign occupiers (mainly Germans and Russians). Today Estonians have a cynical attitude towards authority though their behaviour is always well-mannered. Expectations of leaders are at present a mix of Scandinavian participative management style and a more paternalistic approach, where the leader has to show clear vision and make all the important decisions. Estonia is a transition country where some managers might be very young. A 35-40 year-old person might start his/her second career as an entrepreneur, after he/she has retired from the management board of, for example, a bank.

Latvia

Like their neighbours to the north, Latvians are highly individualistic and are reluctant to follow the crowd. Everybody wants to be not so much a leader as a manager in his/her own right. However there is a tendency to respect firm, confident, knowledgeable leadership; Latvians also always want to be on the side that is winning. They are sometimes reluctant to show initiative. The Germanic influence may explain some of these organisational characteristics.

Lithuania

The influence of the Soviet period is such that Lithuanian organisations function in a rather bureaucratic way. Managers and other employees often "toe the party line" despite a certain resistance to official policies. The older generation of Lithuanian managers have not completely freed themselves of bureaucratic habits from Soviet times, but leadership is developing a more dynamic style among the IT whizz kids and Nordic influence is emphasising this. Lithuanian women are beginning to play vigorous roles in business and politics.

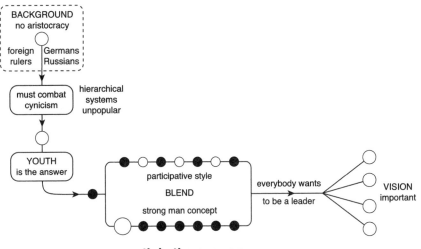

youth is the answer

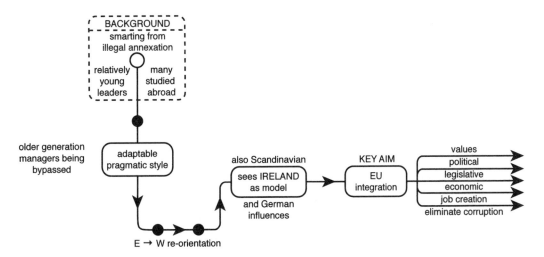

East to West reorientation

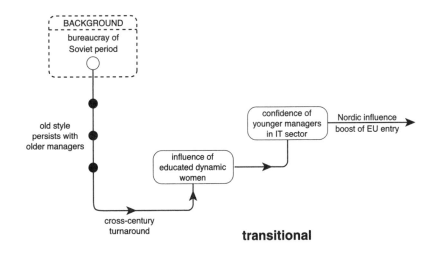

transitional

Poland

In Polish history, royals and nobles have figured largely as leaders and organizers. Gentry comprised a high percentage of feudal society and established a chivalrous, romanticist life style which has a certain identity with Polish national traits. Honour and revenge are living concepts in the Polish mind, as are grace, nobleness of bearing, personal integrity and fearlessness. In these respects they bear comparison with Sicilians and Spaniards. The sense of personal dignity is such that foreigners would do well to impute the best motives to Polish behaviour and be on their guard against offending Poles' sensitivity to remarks which may cause unwitting affront. In more recent years, Nazi suppression and 45 years of communism have diminished the influence of the leading Polish families. Lech Walesa eventually emerged as a working class leader of deeply nationalistic convictions. Meritocracy now dominates advancement in Polish society, though naturally the Polish Pope wielded enormous influence.

Hungary

Under their old aristocracy, Hungarians were often led the wrong way. A conspicuous absence of military victories and political triumphs has made Hungarians adopt a cynical attitude to any kind of leadership. The Soviet rule did nothing to change this attitude. A nation of individualists, Hungarians have gained and encourage status in intellectual, artistic and scientific achievements. Teachers, poets, artists, theatre and film directors, musicians, composers, etc., are well respected, though hardly properly remunerated.

The Czech Republic

The Czech people lost their native nobility in 1648 when they were executed and eliminated by the Habsburgs. Czechs resent power imposed from the outside and never accepted inequality imposed by foreign rulers. The high rate of literacy and general excellence of education over the centuries have enabled Czechs to acquire and enjoy knowledge. Egalitarianism and democratic institutions are instinctively desired. Liberty is seen as something which may be assured by laws, procedures and regulations. Orderliness in society has long been a characteristic of Czech society, though this has often led to excessive officialdom and periods of stifling bureaucracy.

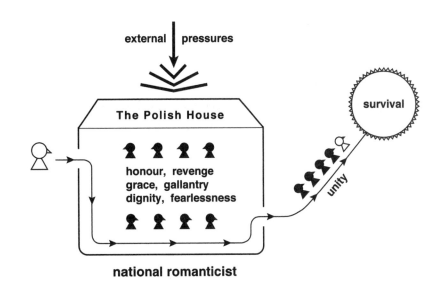

external | **pressures**

The Polish House

honour, revenge
grace, gallantry
dignity, fearlessness

unity

survival

national romanticist

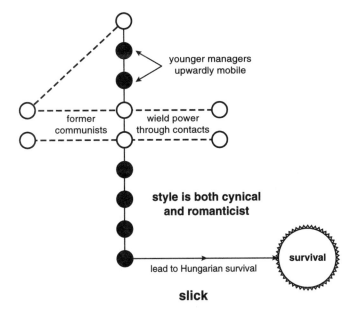

younger managers
upwardly mobile

former
communists

wield power
through contacts

**style is both cynical
and romanticist**

lead to Hungarian survival

survival

slick

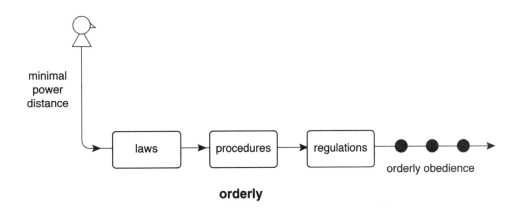

minimal
power
distance

laws → procedures → regulations

orderly obedience

orderly

Slovakia

Slovakia is in transition from Communist rule to a market economy. Former Communist officials have lost leadership positions in general, though a certain number of them have transformed their former political influence into executive power. They had the necessary contacts in many areas of government and economy. Younger managers are on the way up, though an autocratic style is favoured over a consensual one. Few people are anxious to embrace responsibility. Those that are willing to do so may wield their power fairly openly. Before the First World War, leaders were often aristocratic and forceful, but usually Hungarian.

Bulgaria

Bulgaria has no hereditary nobles and consequently social barriers are few. A wide range of people can aspire to leadership, though this depended on Party affiliation from 1945-90. No outstanding political or business leaders have emerged in the last decade. National pessimism and self-doubt hinder the development of political leaders. In business, the future Bulgarian manager is likely to be less autocratic than Serbian or Greek top executives.

Romania

Romania is situated in that part of Europe which was inhabited by peasant masses, ruled for centuries by sovereign lords, clan leaders and autocrats. They held the power of life and death over their underlings. Being themselves the law, they were above the law. They were all-powerful and went unpunished. From ancient times these people were the objects of a blind and slavish worship. Ceausescu belonged to that very tradition. In the post-Ceausescu period, modern leadership styles are hampered in their development, since the government is still run by former communist leaders, who function under other labels. Business leaders are also affected by the continuing influence of the political apparatus. Romanian managers will gradually develop a style of their own – most likely it will resemble that of Italian managers: autocratic but paternalistic and using emotion as a manipulative tool.

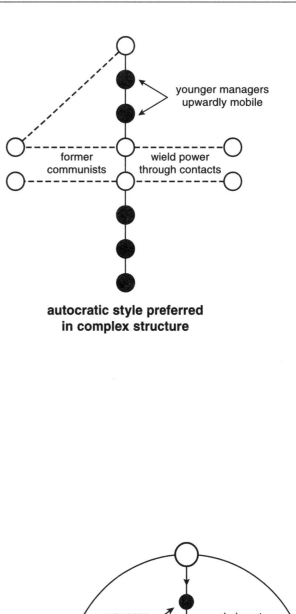

**autocratic style preferred
in complex structure**

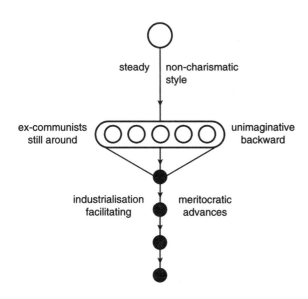

backward leadership

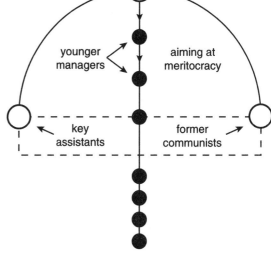

hampered development of leadership

Serbia & Montenegro

The Serb aristocracy and nobility was more or less eradicated by the Ottomans and Turkish dominance over Serbian peasants ensued for the next 500 years. Leadership concepts between the World Wars leant heavily on nationalistic issues and the Second World War left Tito in sole charge. He was a Croat, but represented all Yugoslavs and maintained authority in the fragmented nation successfully until his death. Leadership then was dictated by the needs and demands of each region. Serbian leaders were dictatorial – Milosevic being the prime example. In Serbia, the man in power can get away with a lot.

Slovenia

The Slovenes were governed by the Austrian Habsburgs from the 13th century until 1918. In that year Slovenia became part of the Kingdom of the Serbs, Croats and Slovenes, which was named Yugoslavia in 1929. Leadership began in the Courts and filtered downwards through Court officials. Often in their history, Slovenes have been denied the right to rule themselves. After the Second World War, leadership was invested in Belgrade and practised according to rank in the Communist Party. Since 1992 Slovene leaders have arisen among non-Communist coalition politicians, characterised more by pragmatism than idealism or rhetoric. There is little of the flamboyance displayed by Serbian and even Croatian leaders. In business and academia, qualifications set standards. Orderliness in society is seen as important. Gradually Western European-style democracy is taking hold.

Croatia

Croatia was used by the Habsburgs as a defensive outpost against the Ottoman Empire. Croatian loyalty was to the Habsburg Emperor and to the Catholic Church. Leadership until independence emanated chiefly from Imperial or Church officials. During 45 years of Communism, leadership was invested in Communist party officials, often Serbian. Tito, however, was a Croat. In present-day Croatia, some former Communist luminaries (now converted to a market economy) still linger in the halls of power. The many opportunities offered by tourism, however, are leading to the creation of an entrepreneurial class of managers who embrace Western principles. Meritocracy is on the rise, though respect for status and hierarchical rank remain.

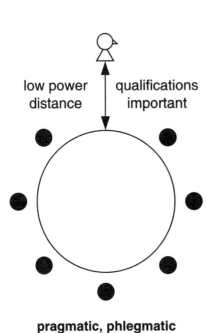

power brokers   ex-communists

vulnerable junior managers

"to have and to hold"

low power   qualifications
distance   important

pragmatic, phlegmatic

"converted"   still
communists   linger

entrepreneurial   developing
managers   quickly

Westernising

Russia

The leadership concept is undergoing profound changes in Russia following the demise of the Soviet Communist state. Efforts made by managers to promote business through official channels only are likely to founder on the rocks of bureaucracy and Russian apathy. Using key people and personal alliances, the "system" is often **by-passed** and a result achieved.

Ukraine

The Ukrainian concept of leadership is derived from many widely differing styles in history. The word "Ukraine" means "borderland" and many races, both nomadic and settlers, have had their turn in dominating this region. In antiquity, Scythians ruled (700-200 B.C.). The golden Age of Kiev (Kievan Rus) was 800-1100 A.D. when Vladimir the Great turned Ukraine towards Byzantine Christianity. The rule of the Polish-Lithuanian Commonwealth pushed the country towards Catholicism, though the peasants remained East Orthodox. Later, the Cossacks (fiercely Orthodox) pushed Ukraine towards Russia. Huge civilian losses in the Second World War and the Great Famine of 1946-47 (caused by the Soviets) led to the Declaration of Independence in 1991. The Ukrainian leadership style reflects all these influences in its autocracy, political manipulation, tendency towards corruption and its preference for males. West and East Ukrainian managers are polarised according to their political leanings.

Belarus

In a dictatorship, most managerial decisions have a political background or motive. The stultifying influence of Soviet bureaucracy and inefficiency has not been completely eradicated from the Belarusian business scene. Leadership, even when non-political, is of the old-fashioned autocratic kind, power distance is steadfastly maintained, consensus is rarely sought enthusiastically and female leaders are few.

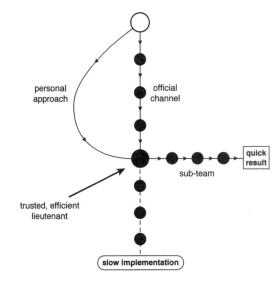

devious management

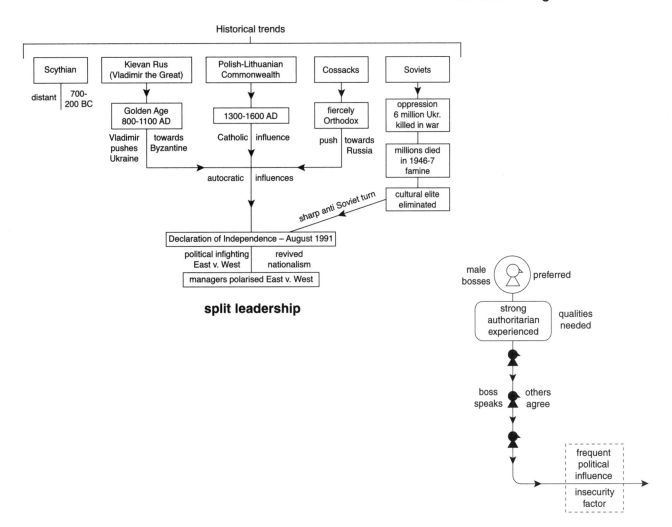

split leadership

political autocracy

Turkey

Kemal Ataturk himself has of course emerged as the model Turkish leader – brave, firm, decisive, innovative, above all humane and commonsensical. His personality was so strong that for decades the majority of Turks, and particularly the Army, have remained loyal to his precepts. It is true that the Army have acted undemocratically on some occasions, seeing themselves as "the guardians of the nation", but after each coup they have handed control back to the civilians.

Iran

In general terms, spiritual leadership is dominant. When the spiritual leader Ayatollah Khomeini decided that it was time for the Shah to step down, support was massive and immediate (over 98%). In business, the leader may be identified as the last person to enter the room at a meeting, and he (and it will be a "he") will sit in the middle. Alternatively, he may show his hospitality by greeting the visitors at the entrance to the room. Academic achievement is of high importance: in government the Iranian leader must be a "fully qualified theologian", selected by "experts". In business, education and specialised knowledge give managers status. Managers may have been educated in the West as well as in Iran.

Israel

Lacking an aristocracy, Israeli society attaches importance to achievement and dynamism when looking for leadership. The troubled time with Israel's Palestinian neighbours since 1945 has led to an enhanced role for the military and hawkish politicians, though the Israeli centre and left have not been without their charismatic figures. It is hard to judge how a period of prolonged peace would affect Israel's choice of leaders. The present hostile situation means that the choice cannot be divorced from political and security-bound realities. It is likely that in less troubled times cultural luminaries would be in the ascendancy, given the level of Israeli education. Religious leaders also exert considerable influence on Israeli life.

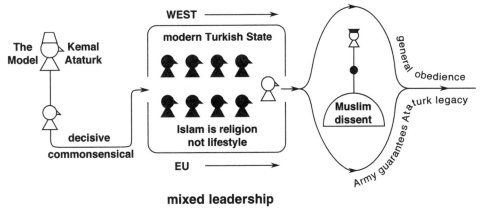

mixed leadership

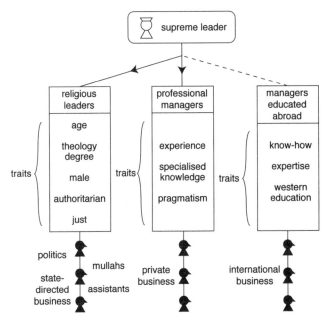

theological ... professional

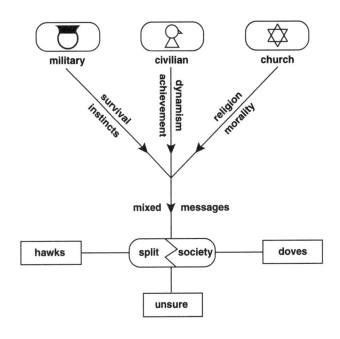

multiple leadership

Iraq

Leadership in today's Iraq is both multifaceted and confused. In Iraq, leadership was in the hands of a despot and his Sunni clique. It seems likely that an important element of future leadership will be the Shiite clergy, though not so powerful as their Iranian colleagues. A pragmatic coalition of Shiites, Sunnis and Kurds is a desirable goal, but extremely difficult to realise on account of bitter sectarianism.

Egypt

Leadership in Egypt has many strands evolving from the autocratic rule of the Pharaohs for many centuries as well as the monarchy in the first part of the 20th century. Nasser's *coup d'état* changed concepts of leadership and Sadat and Mubarak paid lip service to democratic ideals. Dictators, the Islamic church and the military jostle for influence. Business leaders draw on great experience and try, not always successfully, to avoid politics. Nepotism is frequent. Many Egyptian managers have been educated in Britain and the West.

Arab countries (in general)

Arab leaders are often sheikhs and people connected with royal families. There is consequently a lot of nepotism in Arab companies where sons, nephews and brothers hold key positions. This applies particularly in the Gulf States. In other Arab countries dictators influence business leadership – often the military is involved.

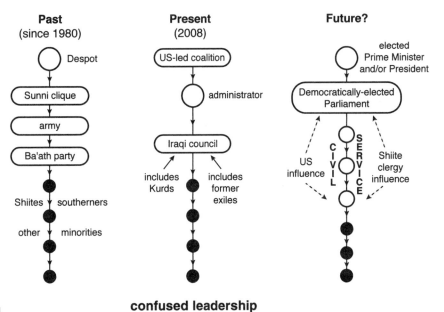

Past
(since 1980)

Despot

Sunni clique

army

Ba'ath party

Shiites southerners

other minorities

Present
(2008)

US-led coalition

administrator

Iraqi council

includes includes
Kurds former
exiles

Future?

elected
Prime Minister
and/or President

Democratically-elected
Parliament

CIVIL SERVICE

US Shiite
influence clergy
influence

confused leadership

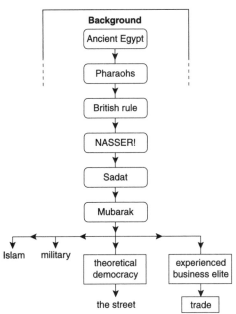

Background

Ancient Egypt

Pharaohs

British rule

NASSER!

Sadat

Mubarak

Islam military theoretical experienced
democracy business elite

the street trade

evolving leadership

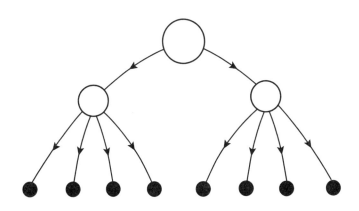

nepotism

Central Asia
Azerbaijan, Kazakhstan, Uzbekistan, Kyrgyzstan, Tajikistan, Turkmenistan

Leadership styles varied among six countries with 50-60 million people spread out over a huge area between the Black Sea and the Chinese border. The Kazakhs, for instance, were rarely united as one nation and they, like Turkmen and Kyrgyz, owed allegiance to nomadic chiefs. Between 1918 and 1991, the Communist Party – directed by the Soviet Union – led the Republics. After the Soviet demise, opportunist dictators seized power and encouraged personality cults. Religious leaders enjoy current influence, especially in Tajikistan and Turkmenistan, less so in Kazakhstan. Kyrgyz leaders are anti-Russian and try to follow the Turkish model of democracy. Turkmenistan is more of a tribal confederation rather than a modern nation. Tajik leaders are often anti-Uzbek. Leaders are aware that throughout the area there are three levels of personal identity: tribal, national and pan-Turkestani. Leadership is consequently complex and often subtle.

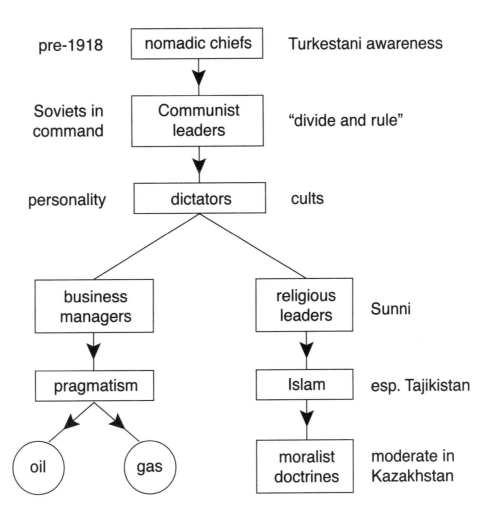

pre-1918	nomadic chiefs	Turkestani awareness
Soviets in command	Communist leaders	"divide and rule"
personality	dictators	cults

business managers → pragmatism → oil, gas

religious leaders (Sunni) → Islam (esp. Tajikistan) → moralist doctrines (moderate in Kazakhstan)

India

Indians accept a hierarchical system with its obligations and duties. The boss must be humanistic and initiate promotion for his subordinates. In family businesses the elder son rarely decides what he wants to be – he is born to carry on the trade of the father. The father is expected to groom him for the job. First a good education will be provided. The son must study hard – then the next step will be indicated. In the political sphere, India is the world's largest democracy. Leadership involves both the President and Parliament, but sectarian disputes are frequent. The Muslim minority (c. 160 million) are however properly represented in Parliament.

Pakistan

Since independence, Pakistan has been officially a democracy with a Parliament and supporting institutions. In practice, the country has been ruled by the military, or civilian despots. Business leaders, as in India, function in a hierarchical style, but have to accept certain constraints imposed by the military and, increasingly, Islamic leaders. Within these same constraints, nepotism is frequent.

Bangladesh

In its brief history, Bangladesh has been led by very different figures. The first Prime Minister, Sheikh Mujib, was known as the Father of the Nation, echoing the reputation of Nehru in neighbouring India. He, like Nehru, favoured secularism as the most suitable path for a state which featured diverse faiths and considerable tribalism. He was assassinated. The following two leaders, Zia and Ershad, were dictators. Rule, though administered by political parties, was in effect despotic.

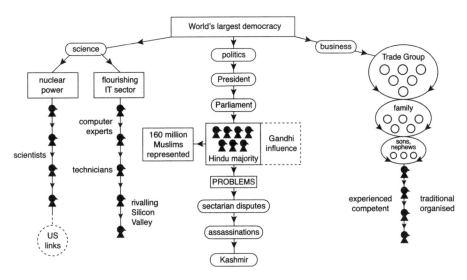

multi-faceted leadership

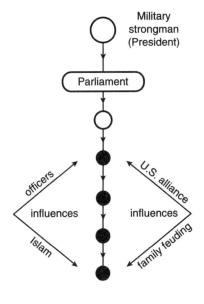

fragile, volatile

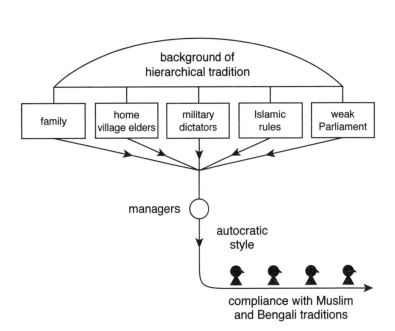

Bengali & Muslim

Japan

Japanese top executives have great power in conformity with Confucian hierarchy, but actually have little involvement in the everyday affairs of the company. On appropriate occasions they initiate policies which are conveyed to middle managers and rank and file. Ideas often originate on the factory floor or with other lower level sources. Signatures are collected among workers and middle managers as suggestions, ideas and inventions make their way up the company hierarchy ("ringi-sho" system). Many people are involved. Top executives take the final step in ratifying items that have won sufficient approval.

China

Consensus is generally highly valued in China, but in companies controlled by the state a leadership group (often invisible) will decide policy. In the developing expansion of capitalist-style companies, leaders are emerging with reputations of competence, also locally-elected officials (e.g. mayors) are becoming influential in the business sphere and may have only loose ties with Beijing. In Chinese family businesses (and there are many) the senior male is the patriarch and the usual nepotic structure is observable.

Hong Kong

Politically, consensus is generally highly valued in Hong Kong, but in companies autocracy is the norm. Leaders with competence may have only loose ties with Beijing. In Chinese family businesses (and there are many) the senior male is the patriarch and the usual nepotic structure is observable. Management style has changed surprisingly little since reunification. Decisions are speedy, red tape is anathema.

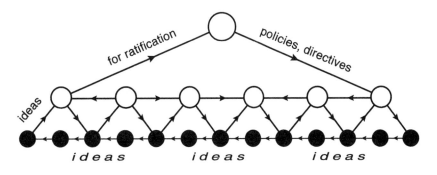

ringi-sho consensus

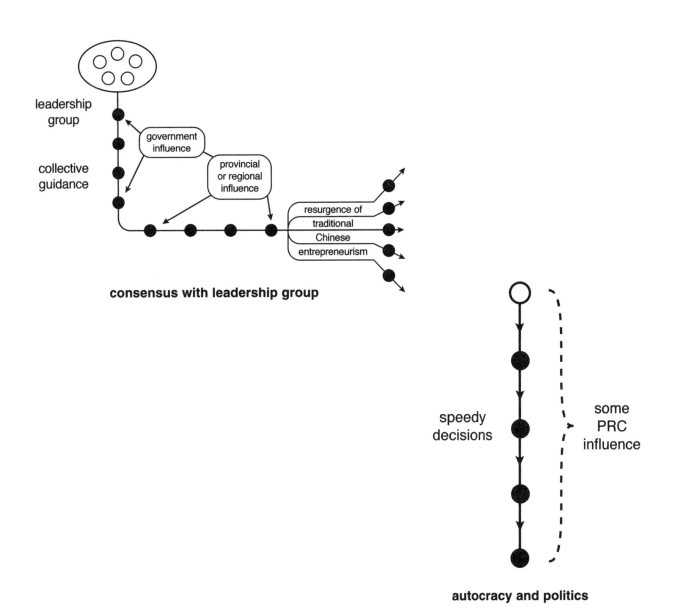

leadership
group

collective
guidance

government
influence

provincial
or regional
influence

resurgence of
traditional
Chinese
entrepreneurism

consensus with leadership group

speedy
decisions

some
PRC
influence

autocracy and politics

South Korea

"Chaebols" (conglomerates) control a lot of business in Korea. These were, and are, family-owned and nepotism is rampant with all sons, brothers, nephews, etc., holding key positions. The very size of these conglomerates has, however, necessitated the introduction of a class of professional managers. These are now ubiquitous and growing in importance. Decision-making is therefore largely hybrid, nevertheless fairly quick.

North Korea

Leadership in North Korea is practised according to the Juche concept, which is a strange combination of Stalinism and Asian implacability. It emanates from the philosophies and teachings of Kim Il-sung, the father of Kim Jong-il, the current dictator. No political ideas or discussions are allowed which do not conform with Juche dogma and doctrine. Leadership is therefore embedded in coercion and is based on hatred of Western decadence (which, in North Korean eyes, South Korea shares).

The Philippines

Filipinos are proud of their democracy, but have suffered at the hands of dictators, particularly Ferdinand Marcos. Other leaders in recent times have been a general (Fidel Ramos), a housewife (Corazón Aquino) and a film star (Estrada). Filipino managers pay lip service to the democratic ideal, but are rather autocratic in their management style. They maintain a considerable power distance vis-à-vis subordinates. Paternalism is common and employees may ask superiors to help them with various matters. Older people are expected to give advice to younger ones, who listen to them attentively. Managers must give clear instructions to achieve progress.

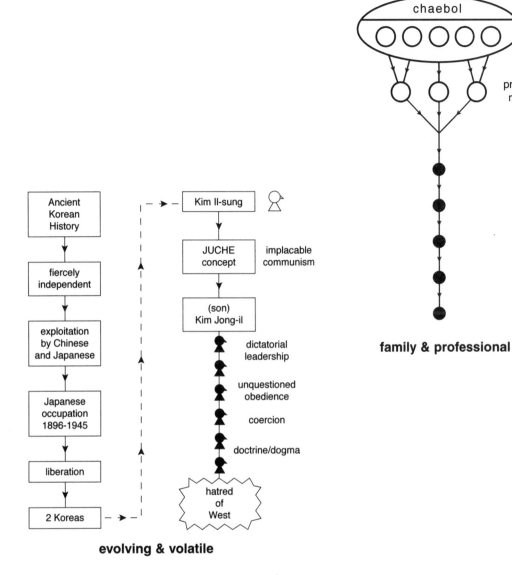

chaebol

professional managers

family & professional

Ancient Korean History

fiercely independent

exploitation by Chinese and Japanese

Japanese occupation 1896-1945

liberation

2 Koreas

Kim Il-sung

JUCHE concept — implacable communism

(son) Kim Jong-il

dictatorial leadership

unquestioned obedience

coercion

doctrine/dogma

hatred of West

evolving & volatile

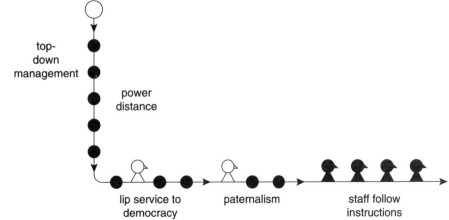

top-down management

power distance

lip service to democracy

paternalism

staff follow instructions

democratic autocracy

Thailand

Questions of leadership are easily resolved in Thailand. In 1257 the Kingdom of Sukhothai adopted the paternalistic system of government. The King, while enjoying absolute sovereign power, would, like a father, look after his subjects and personally pay close attention to their well-being. The Khmer system had been based on the concept of Divine Right (not unlike England's). The bloodless coup of 1932 which led to Thailand changing from absolute to constitutional monarchy, did little to alter this privilege. Today the King's power emanates from the people, he is Head of State and of the armed forces and upholder of Buddhism and all other religions. In Thailand authority and power are considered natural to the human condition. The holder of power has accumulated merit in a previous life. The best leader (also in business) is one who empathises most with his subordinates.

Vietnam

Tradition is one of a collective leadership according to Confucian tenets. Currently, leaders must possess a good war record and adhere to socialist thinking. Before Chinese rule (beginning in 100 B.C.), old Vietnamese society was organised along hierarchical feudal lines. Tribal chiefs – civil, religious and military – were often large landowners and controlled serfs. Power was hereditary. A shogun-like figure was usually "king". This societal structure showed strong affinities with the Mon-Khmer, Tai and Melano-Indonesian peoples (not the Chinese). Managers in the south are more Westernised.

Myanmar

Leadership in everyday life is currently in the hands of the frequently superstitious generals, who ruthlessly suppress any political opposition. For decades they have dictated the fortunes of the country in spite of fierce international criticism and being completely out of step with the other countries in the region. Most business decisions are taken by officials who toe the government line or who are themselves in uniform. The military often aligns itself with Theravada Buddhism in an attempt to cultivate an aura of respectability and decency in this overwhelmingly devout nation.

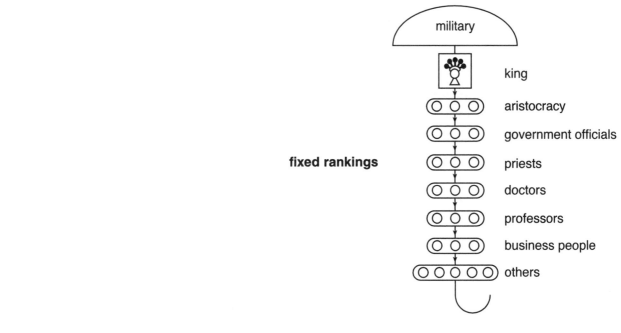

fixed rankings

- military
- king
- aristocracy
- government officials
- priests
- doctors
- professors
- business people
- others

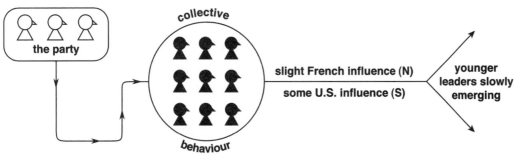

the party

collective

behaviour

slight French influence (N)

some U.S. influence (S)

younger leaders slowly emerging

slowly Westernising

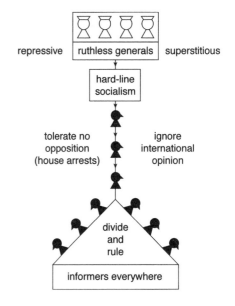

repressive   ruthless generals   superstitious

hard-line socialism

tolerate no opposition (house arrests)

ignore international opinion

divide and rule

informers everywhere

socialism + Buddhism + superstition

Singapore

30 years of skilful leadership by the "benevolent despot" Lee Kuan Yew converted the disputatious, multi-racial community of Singapore into a disciplined, prosperous state of 4 million people with a per capita GDP approaching $30,000 (2007). Lee had a firm hand, leading autocratically with an agenda of law and order, strict discipline, health and sanitation controls, hard work and elimination of corruption. Managers continue largely in his image and there are few dissenters. One can set up a business in six days. The country is still multi-racial, but the Chinese community dominates and observes basically Confucian tenets, spiced up a little with linear-active Western concepts.

Indonesia

Leaders are usually from chosen families or emanate from the higher ranks in the army, and are expected to be paternalistic. They often seek consensus, which is the mode followed by everyone. In colonial times, leadership came from the Dutch. Under Sukarno and Suharto leadership was exercised principally by the military and was therefore autocratic. The indifferent nature of many Indonesians to the business process, has, however, resulted in a lot of business management being entrusted to a resident Chinese professional class, which has the commercial know-how and international connections. Overseas Chinese shareholding in many Indonesian companies encourages this situation.

Malaysia

People born in high positions are expected to demonstrate leadership capabilities. A good leader is religiously devout, sincere, humble and tactful. Status is inherited, not earned, confirmed by demonstrating leadership and a caring attitude. Malays feel comfortable in a hierarchical structure in which they have a definite role. Work and idleness are not clearly delineated in Malay culture and language. Work is only one of many activities pursued by the Malays. Deepening of relationships and time spent with the elderly may be seen as idle pursuits by Westerners, not by Malays. Malays are modest and rarely request promotion. They expect it to be accorded by a caring senior when the time is ripe.

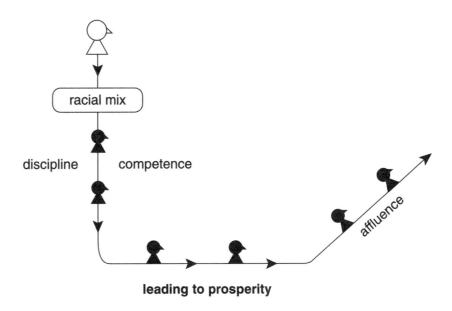

leading to prosperity

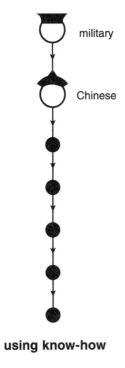

using know-how

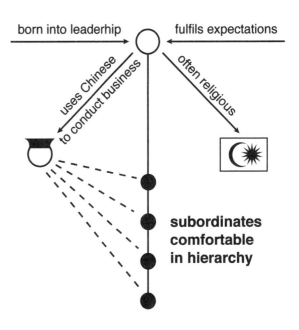

gently hierarchical

French North Africa

Leader types vary across North Africa from the Royal Family in Morocco to dictators in Tunisia and multi-party rule in Algeria, where the army is always a force to be reckoned with. Bourguiba encouraged westernisation in Tunisia, and all ex-French colonies follow this trend, especially senior executives. There is a growing professional managerial class, almost entirely Muslim, but French-influenced in terms of hierarchical structure in companies and task management. Women are considerably westernised, but do not have a significant role in the upper echelons of business.

Portuguese Africa

Leadership and positions of influence derive largely from the individuals who came out on top after the civil war. Politicians and some civil servants acquired considerable wealth and they have their own following in wielding power in both the economic and political sphere. In rural areas leaders, traditionally, are elderly men with prominent lineage in their tribe. Tribal factions weigh heavily on aspects of leadership even in the cities. Normal African hierarchies are of course considerably distorted by the wealth question.

Sub-Saharan Africa

Traditionally, many societies were based on clans and lineages, with most authority being held by genealogically senior men. Clans might consist of a single kinship unit, but would be linked with neighbouring tribes/groups by ties of intermarriage and consciousness of common cultural identity. This type of leadership still exists, but economic change, where Africa has become part of the total worldwide system of economic production and exchange, has weakened clan and tribal influence. The traditional equality of living standards has been affected, especially in the cities, by the growth of new élites and the appearance of a poor and typically exploited urban proletariat.

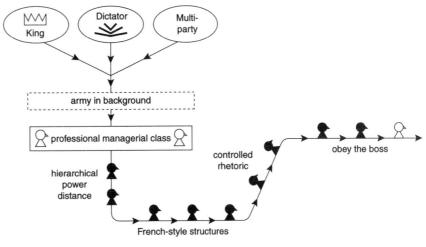

Gallicised

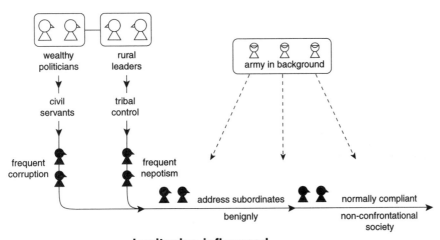

Lusitanian-influenced

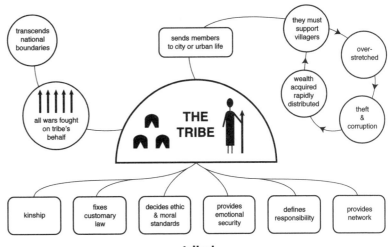

tribal

South Africa (black)

Using Nelson Mandela as a model, African leaders find him a hard act to follow, in view of his unique skills in leading from the front (even in jail), his disarming manner and all-encompassing perspective. Current leadership is often beset by factional problems. The flock is by no means docile or unified. So far democratic methods have enjoyed success and irremedial confrontation with the whites has been avoided. The gradual emergence of a sizeable black middle class has facilitated steadiness and continuity.

South Africa (white British)

The British South African community possesses business and political leaders of considerable perspicacity. Cultural sensitivity is generally a strong point and in this respect they compare well with Europeans. They often show a good grasp of human nature and are comfortable in managerial situations. They are usually excellent arbitrators, using gentle persuasion to achieve their goals.

South Africa (white Dutch)

Afrikaner business and political leaders are characterised by their boldness and directness. Cultural sensitivity is generally a strong point and in this respect they compare well with Europeans. In conformity with their history, Afrikaners relish commanding and assume responsibility with gusto. They are clever in varying their leadership style according to which cultural group their staff belong.

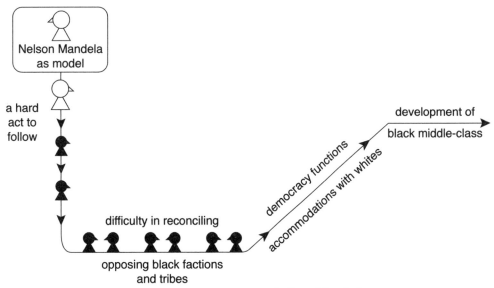

follow Mandela

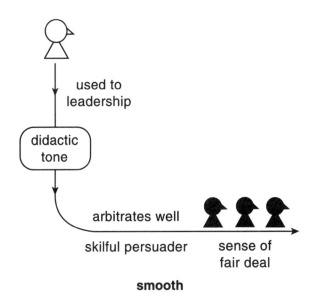

smooth

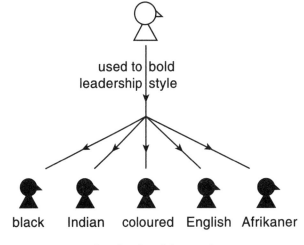

varies leadership mode

Australia

Australian managers, like Swedes, must sit in the ring with the "mates". From this position, once it is accepted that they will not pull rank, they actually exert much more influence than their Swedish counterparts, as the semi-Americanized nature of Australian business requires quick thinking and rapid decision-making. There lingers considerable irreverence among Australians for figures in authority. Pompous leaders (and there are not many) are rapidly cut down in conformity with the "tall poppy syndrome".

New Zealand

Most New Zealanders are brought up to respect authority and managers have a relatively easy task as long as they function in a calm, egalitarian and reasoning manner. Consensus is generally sought before important decisions are made and if things go wrong, leaders are rarely made scapegoats. New Zealand is a very small country with economic disadvantages due to their isolation and "pulling together" is seen as advisable.

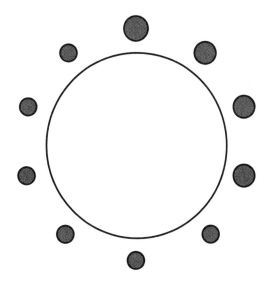

one of the mates

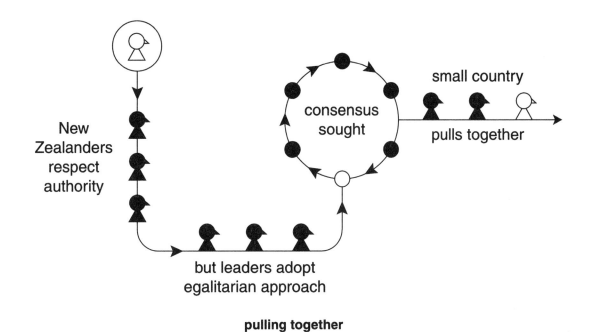

pulling together

USA

American leadership symbolises the vitality and audacity of the land of free enterprise. Management structure is pyramidical, with seniors driving and inspiring people under them. Americans are allowed to make individual decisions, but usually within the framework of corporate restrictions. Managers are capable of teamwork and corporate spirit, but value individual freedom more than company welfare. They are very mobile. They get fired if they make mistakes.

Canada

In English-speaking Canada, leading statesmen are generally low key. Not many non-Canadians can remember the name of any Canadian premier except perhaps Pierre Trudeau. Québécois leaders have, naturally, more Gallic flair. In business, Canadian managers behave in a subdued manner in comparison with their American counterparts and are expected by their staff to be truthful, trusting and egalitarian. Though results-oriented, their route to success is governed by common sense rather than aggressive methods.

Mexico

The Mexican leader is a family man and a good Catholic; his shrewdness and skills in business are not allowed to intrude upon this basic goodness. His subordinates, aware of his completeness, obey him without question. They know that he has to reciprocate their willingness by his own loyalty, courtesy, compassion and protection towards them. The similarity with the comportment of Japanese managers and staff is striking (probably not unrelated to the Asian provenance of American Indians!).

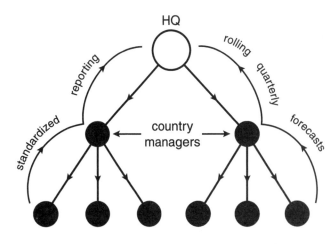

upper/middle managers make individual decisions

structured individualism

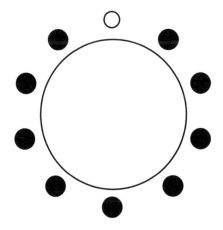

low-key dynamo

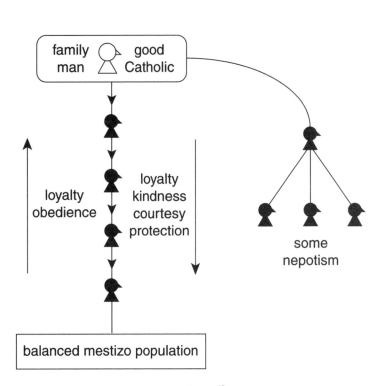

paternalism

Hispanic America (in general)

Leadership in most Hispanic American countries has traditionally been centred around a strong dictator or military figure or, in the case of Mexico and Argentina, dominant political parties. Nepotism is common and staff are manipulated by a variety of persuasive methods ranging from (benign) paternalism to outright exploitation and coercion.

Brazil

Leaders in Brazil have often been military officers or civilian strongmen ruling with the approval of the army. The huge size of the economy has in recent years generated a large professional class which regulates the conduct of business on a day-to-day basis. The volatility of the economy often necessitates state interference. Managers normally rule in an autocratic manner, but often strive to be encouraging, even cheerful, vis-à-vis subordinates.

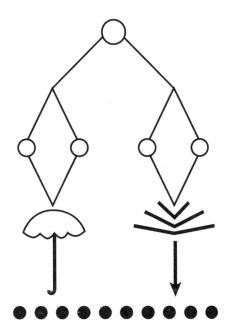

paternalism & coercion

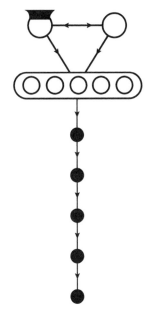

political ... professional

Cuba

Castroism is the order of the day and dominates all levels of political activity as well as managerial style. There is little latitude for managers to deviate from the official line, so originality in decision-making or introducing innovation is at a minimum.

Jamaica

It is hard to define the exact qualities that Jamaicans look for in a leader, since they want "strong men" but often vote them out of office when they take tough decisions. Trade unions are very strong, though many leaders stay in office too long and fail to implement many of their goals. A new female Prime Minister with evangelical charisma proved popular. Warmth, as well as strength, is expected from a leader.

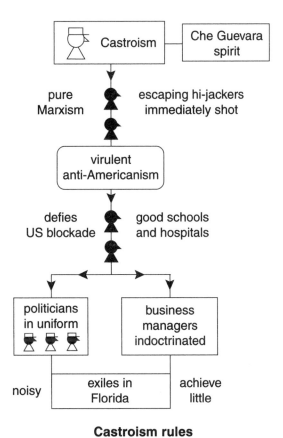

Castroism rules

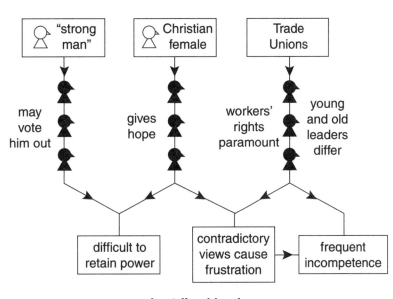

short-lived leaders

Exercises

1 | **What is your own leadership style like? Describe it briefly in words below:**

-
-
-
-
-
-
-

2 | **Now draw a diagram to describe your leadership style in the space below, combining words and visuals:**

3 Flick through the leadership style diagrams on pages 137-189. Which cultures are you most similar to and which ones do you differ from? Write them down below:

Similar

-
-
-
-
-

Different

-
-
-
-
-

4 Think about managers you have had in the past. Describe the leadership qualities of one you liked and one you disliked:

The qualities of a leader you liked:

-
-
-
-
-

The qualities of a leader you disliked:

-
-
-
-
-

5 Think about people you have led / managed in the past. Why were some people difficult to lead and how could you adjust your leadership style to manage them?

Characteristics of "difficult" subordinates:

-
-
-
-

I could adjust my leadership style by:

-
-
-
-

6 Do you have any current problems leading or being led?
Visit **www.crossculture.com/visualapproach**, describe your situation, and we will provide some advice.

Language of Management

Among the tasks of managers are the necessities of instructing, motivating and leading their subordinates. They may often lead by example, but as far as motivation and the issuance of directives are concerned, they will be heavily dependent on language. Different languages are used in different ways and with a variety of effects. Hyperbolic American and understated British English clearly inform and inspire listening staff with separate allure and driving force. Managers of all nationalities know how to speak to their compatriots to best effect, for there are built-in characteristics in their language which facilitate the conveyance of ideas to their own kind. They are in fact only vaguely aware of their dependence on these linguistic traits which make their job easier. With increasing globalisation, problems will arise in the following instances:

(a) when managers are involved in international team building;
(b) when they have to use a language other than their own.

An example of situation (a) is when a Briton or American addresses a team containing, among others, Germans. The occasional quipping or half-serious remarks typical of Anglo-American managers will only too often be taken literally by Germans, who may carry out "orders" which were only being casually considered.

An example of (b) is when a Japanese managing Anglo-Saxons hints at directives in such a courteous and half-suggestive manner that all is lost in a fog of impeccable politeness. How does the particular genius of a certain language, manifested by its structure, vocabulary and tones, play its part in conveying instructions and inspiration to its listeners? Let us examine some of the characteristics of languages which are tools of management in parts of the industrialized world.

England

In England, language used by managers is a subtle management tool. English staff members, who would be put off by American exaggeration and tough talk, fall for a more understated, laid-back version of English which reflects their own characteristics. Managers manipulate subordinates with friendly small talk, humour, reserved statements of objectives and a very casual approach to getting down to work. You don't arrive on the dot and work round the clock. The variety of types of humour available in England enables managers to be humorous, to praise, change direction, chide, insinuate and criticise at will. They may even level criticism at themselves. Irony is a powerful weapon either way.

Scotland

Scots leaders address subordinates in an inspirational, commanding, yet folksy manner. Their speech is direct and crisp, and orders are clear. There is no "wimpy" or hesitant tone in Scots language of management. Strong Scots traditions and occasional bursts of nationalism unite leaders and staff. Scots working for managers in the south of England often complain of "woolly directives". Scots rival Germans and Finns in directness and avoidance of ambiguity.

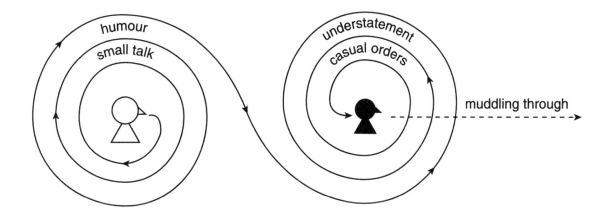

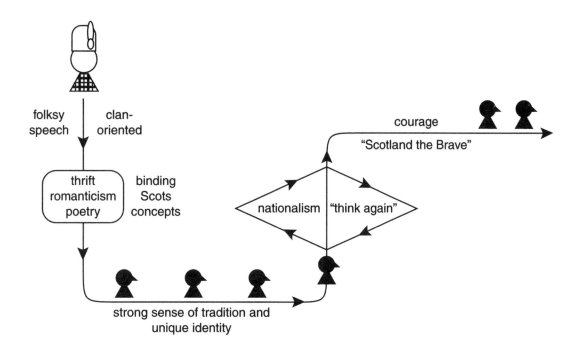

Ireland

Irish managers, like Australians, are often expected to speak with a broad, local accent to make their subordinates feel close to them. While a few Irish speak something close to southern English, most lead with the charming Irish lilt which even English people find attractive and disarming. It has a subtle music deriving from the tones of Gaelic, unfortunately no longer used in business. Irish leaders, like Poles and Spaniards, apply a poetic touch to their dialogue and command allegiance through a skilful combination of ironic humour, subtle references and reasonable proposals. Embellishment and some hyperbole (but not hype) are expected and offered.

Wales

Whether English or the Welsh language is used, managers address their staff in a folksy way without any trace of superior airs. When using English, the language may be very broad. The Welsh, like the Irish, have an artistic, poetic bent and mild nationalism may be evident when they are dealing with English people. There is generally a lot of human contact between Welsh managers and their staff members.

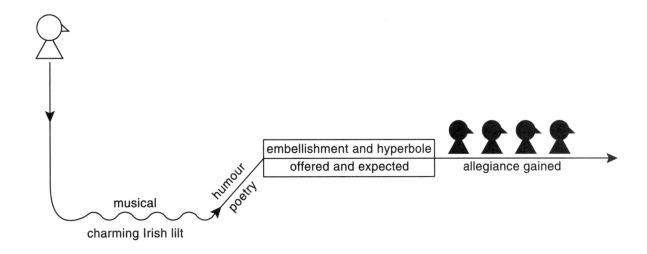

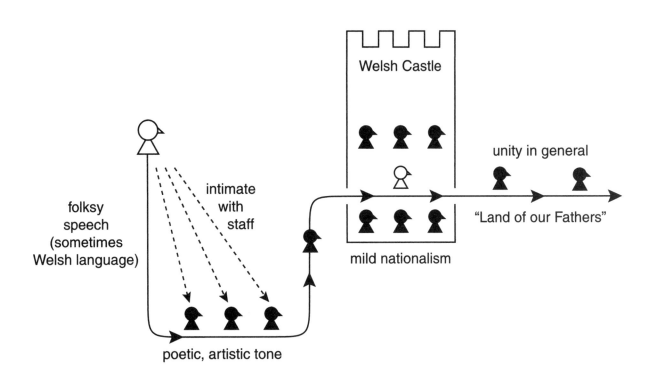

Germany

Germans belong to a data-oriented, low context culture and like receiving detailed information and instruction to guide them in the performance of tasks at which they wish to excel. In business situations German is not used in a humorous way, neither do its rigid case-endings and strict word order allow the speaker to think aloud very easily. With few homonyms (in contrast, for example, to Chinese) and a transparent word-building system, the language is especially conducive to the issuing of clear orders. The almost invariable use of the formal "Sie" form in business fits in well with the expectation of obedience and reinforces the hierarchical nature of the communication.

Italy

Which adjectives best describe the Italian language, known the world over for its pleasing effect on the ear? Soft, fluent, melodious, elegant, aesthetic, musical, pliant, seductive are some that come to mind. These terms indeed reflect the style of Italian managers as they seek to instruct, influence, persuade and perhaps charm their staff to comply with their requirements. Italians are cultured, finicky listeners who would be alienated by authoritarian German, exaggerated, simplified American, cacophonous gobbled Dutch or glottal Danish. They expect to be addressed with elegance and refinement, to be subtly manipulated, perhaps skilfully cajoled, but always in a medium corresponding to their civilised state, sense of aesthetics and acute awareness. The Italian language, spoken by an educated native, can satisfy all these needs.

France

French is a crisp, incisive tongue, a kind of verbal dance or gymnastics of the mouth, which presses home its points with an undisguised, logical urgency. It is rational, precise and ruthless in its clarity. The French education system, from childhood, places a premium on articulateness and eloquence of expression. In the French culture, loquacity is equated with intelligence and silence does not have a particularly golden sheen. Lycée, university and École Normale Supérieure education reinforces the emphasis on good speaking, purity of grammar and mastery of the French idiom. The French language, unquestionably, is the chief weapon wielded by managers in directing, motivating and dominating their staff. Less articulate French people will show no resentment. Masterful use of language and logic implies, in their understanding, masterful management.

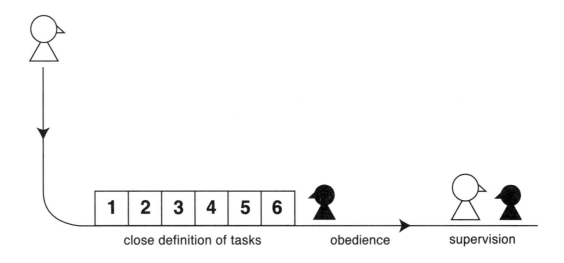

close definition of tasks   obedience   supervision

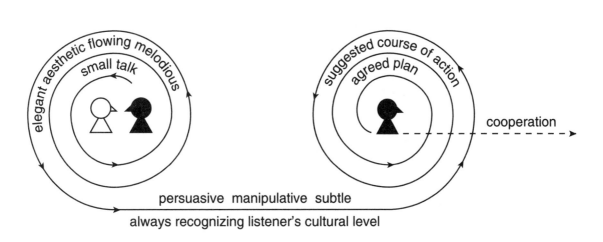

elegant aesthetic flowing melodious

small talk

suggested course of action

agreed plan

cooperation

persuasive manipulative subtle

always recognizing listener's cultural level

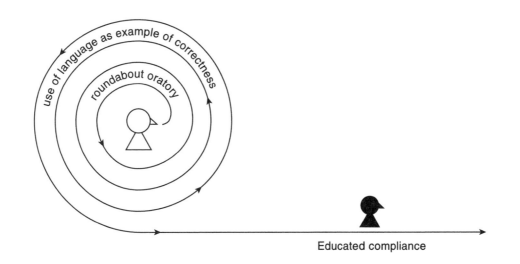

use of language as example of correctness

roundabout oratory

Educated compliance

Switzerland

Swiss managers address their subordinates in four different languages, according to their cultural group. Those using Swiss German ("Schwyzerdütsch") switch to ordinary German, when there are other nationals in the audience (or indeed English). The styles all share Swiss reserve, caution and common sense.

Spain

Spanish is directed towards staff at a rather vertical angle. Spanish managers are usually happy to use the "tu" form (informal) to subordinates, but the declaimed nature of their delivery, with typical Spanish fire and emphasis, makes their pronouncements and opinions virtually irreversible. Spanish, with its wealth of diminutive endings, its rich vocabulary and multiple choice options on most nouns, is extremely suitable for expressing emotion, endearments, nuances and intimacies. Spanish managers' discourse leans on emotive content. They woo, persuade, cajole. They want you to know how they feel. The language exudes warmth, excitement, sensuousness, ardour, ecstasy and sympathy.

The Netherlands

Somewhat guttural Dutch, sister language to German, has a similar disciplined structure but is more folksy and less authoritarian than the latter. The tight grammar, allied to an absence of pretence to elegance, suits the tough, but give-and-take style of the Dutch manager.

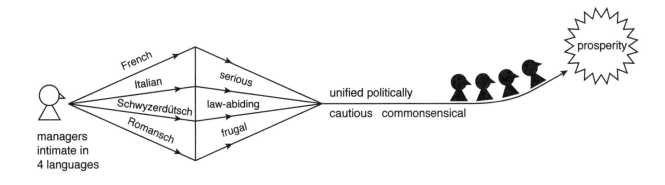

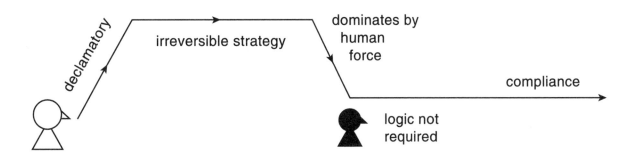

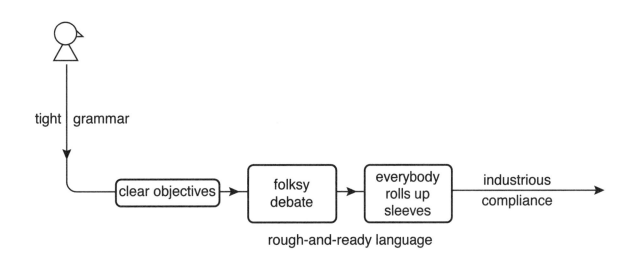

Austria (Vienna)

Austrian managers impress their staff with their command of appropriate language, which, in their case, is a combination of folksy Austrian-accented German (to show solidarity) and sophisticated French loan-words (to show erudition). As in France, elegant speech commands admiration.

Austria (Tirol)

The language of management in the Tirolean part of Austria differs from that of Vienna in its less complex and cosmopolitan style, concentrating on a commonsensical and calm approach to issues dealt with in a disciplined, orderly manner. The strongly-accented local dialects are a unifying factor.

Portugal

Portuguese is a beautiful and extremely sensitive language, containing a greater variety of sounds (particularly vowels, diphthongs and triphthongs) than any other European tongue. Portuguese managers use the language skilfully, with great delicacy and clever use of diminutives, creating an impression of deep human understanding vis-à-vis their staff. It is a language of subtle persuasion and direction and is generally very effective in reaching agreement and compliance.

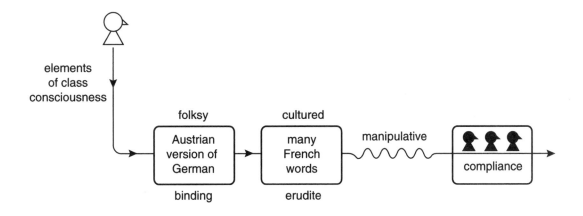

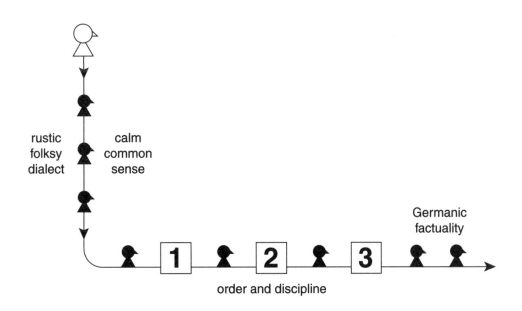

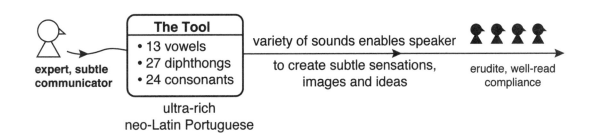

Belgium (Flemish)

Flemish is a Germanic language, disciplined in grammar and with somewhat transparent word building. It lends itself to factual descriptions and clear instructions, which suits down-to-earth Flemish staff.

Belgium (Walloon)

The Walloon language of management resembles the French inasmuch as mastery of the language gives the manager an advantage over, and respect from, less articulate subordinates. The style is humbler than French in France, also suited to the Walloon mentality.

Greece

The Greek management style is typified by loquacious and eloquent leaders who use all the subtleties and nuances of the Greek language to convince their staff of the course to follow. Argument can be intense and lengthy, but always encompasses a certain elegance and softness.

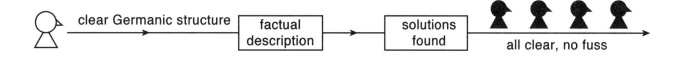

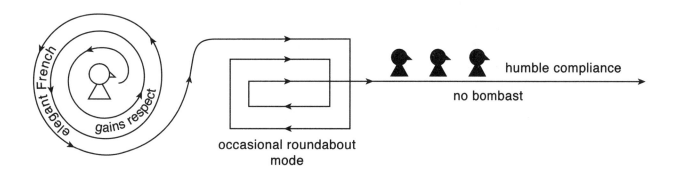

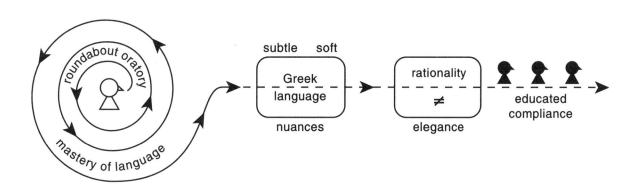

Finland

Finnish management, though basically democratic, differs slightly from that of its Scandinavian neighbours inasmuch as the decisive, strongman type plays a greater role when things get bogged down. Finnish bosses are not averse to blowing hot and cold when they want things from their staff. They can be cold, terse and factual in one mode, then switch to a richer, more flowery one when it suits their purpose. Finnish – an Eastern tongue – is more vibrant and sinewy than Scandinavian languages, with a much richer, adjective-strewn vocabulary, an army of manipulative particles and no fewer than 14 case-endings. These features give the speaker far more linguistic options than one can call on in most languages. Finnish managers are generally well educated, keep richness of expression in reserve in general day-to-day address, but occasionally "pull out all the stops" when praise, encouragement or reprimand are appropriate. Finnish women are more communicative than men.

Sweden

Swedish is the democratic language par excellence. As a language of management, it leans heavily on the informal "du" form and dry, courteous expressions which clearly stratify managers at the same level as their colleagues or, at the very worst, as *primi inter pares*. I recently heard a TV journalist in his mid-twenties address the Prime Minister as "du" (the PM had agreed in advance to this mode of address).

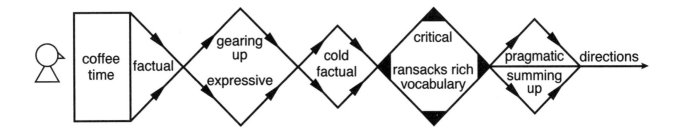

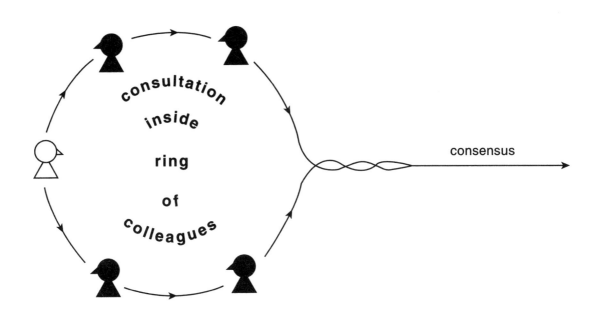

Denmark

Danish is a less strident language than Norwegian and less deliberate than Swedish. It excels in confiding, almost conspiratorial tones, enabling the manager to share ideas in a closely confidential manner with colleagues, among whom he/she mingles. Danish is low-key, calm, serious, but with hidden shafts of humour. It bespeaks long experience and wisdom. The Kingdom of Denmark has been around for over 1,000 years. Controlled organisation and "small-and-quiet is beautiful" is the essence of the tongue.

Norway

Norwegian managers addressing their staff have a strong and effective linguistic tool at their disposal. Spoken Norwegian is brisk, strident and cheerful – it has a fresh-air style about it. The distinctive, emphatic, rising tones of the language emphasize the Norway-centredness of the medium, serving to link managers more closely to their staff. It is not too low-key and hints at great energy. Essentially democratic, the recent standardisation of the language (since the 1950s) enables the manager to identify with all Norwegians and to confirm he/she is "with it".

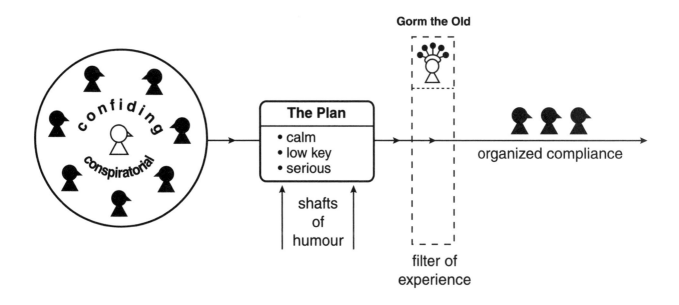

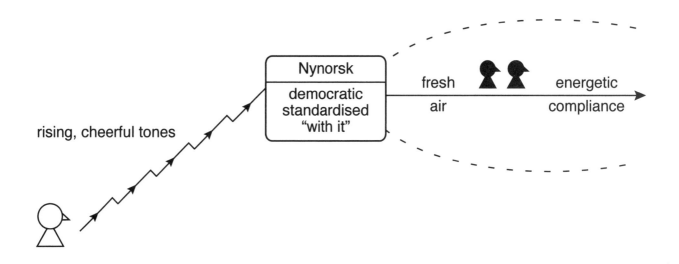

Estonia

The Estonian language is as rich as Finnish, which it resembles. Managers address their staff in a very factual manner, though elegance of vocabulary is admired. The sizeable Russian minority has difficulties with Estonian and the Russian language is used in many cases.

Latvia

Managers address staff in a cool, measured manner, reacting against the former rhetorical style of Russians. They emphasise the use of Latvian as the language of local business and mix optimism with realism. The Russian minority is large, especially in cities.

Lithuania

Lithuanian is a rich, expressive language, enabling managers to revel in its aesthetic, archaic constructions. The fact that Lithuanian is replacing Russian as the principal language of business is satisfying to employees. The Russian minority is small compared to Estonia and Latvia.

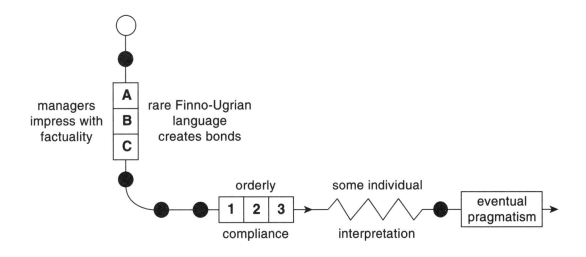

managers impress with factuality

rare Finno-Ugrian language creates bonds

orderly compliance

some individual interpretation

eventual pragmatism

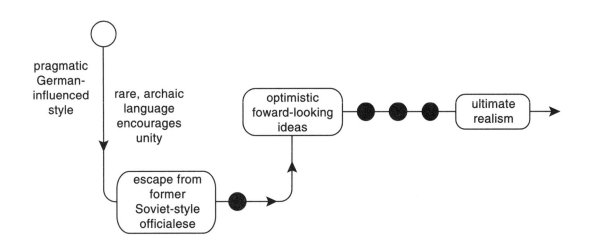

pragmatic German-influenced style

rare, archaic language encourages unity

escape from former Soviet-style officialese

optimistic foward-looking ideas

ultimate realism

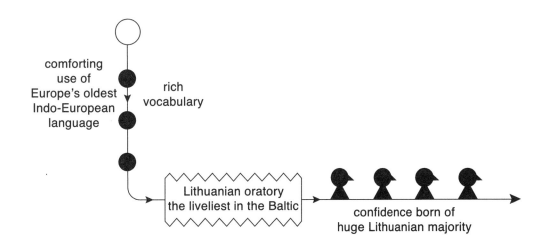

comforting use of Europe's oldest Indo-European language

rich vocabulary

Lithuanian oratory the liveliest in the Baltic

confidence born of huge Lithuanian majority

Poland

Polish is a subtle language which serves managers as a useful tool in motivating their staff. Politeness is inherent in the tongue, as is respect for status at all levels. The language has fire and vibrancy to inspire, but has subtle, endearing terms which appeal to the listener's sentimentality. Managers may use facts and figures to motivate, but the key to the Polish heart is sentimental romanticism – part and parcel of the national tongue – so long a symbol of Polish nationalism and identity. Polish has a rhythmic melodious sound. When wielded by a skilful speaker the language can have a powerfully soothing effect on Polish staff.

Hungary

Hungarians are passionately fond of their own language and are proud of their extensive literature. Successful Hungarian managers are expected to have mastery of the language, which is rich in imagery. They are also expected to talk at length, covering all aspects of challenges to be met. In these respects, the requirements for Hungarian language of management are very similar to the French.

The Czech Republic

Czech is a Slavic language with all the richness of vocabulary that this entails. Managers use the spoken tongue fairly volubly, but without great excitement or emotion. Reasoning and logic predominate. Humour is frequent and welcome.

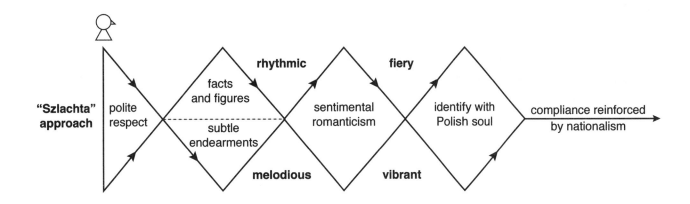

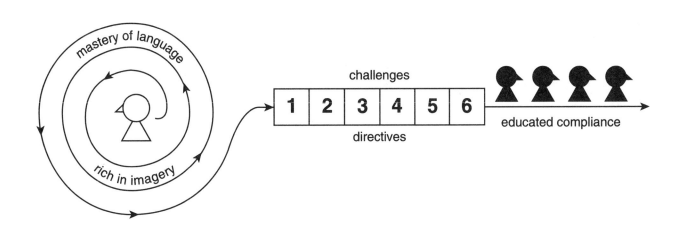

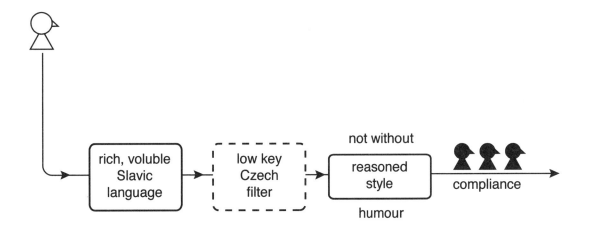

Slovakia

Slovak managers issue orders and expect them to be obeyed. They are quite expressive in their own language and generally gain compliance without difficulty. The richness of the language enables them to be very persuasive when it is necessary. They sell their ideas softly but with tenacity.

Bulgaria

The Bulgarian language is rich in poetry, symbolism and nuance. Bulgarian managers combine these linguistic tools with a compassionate approach to motivation. Bulgarian employees are docile in comparison with Serbs, Croats or Romanians.

Romania

Romanians are naturally proud of their language, given its hybrid specialness. Vocabulary contributions from both Latin and Slavic give the language a greater breadth and richness than either. Managers are able to manipulate and lead staff by means of this excellent and expressive tool. Oratorical ability enhances the whole and commands allegiance.

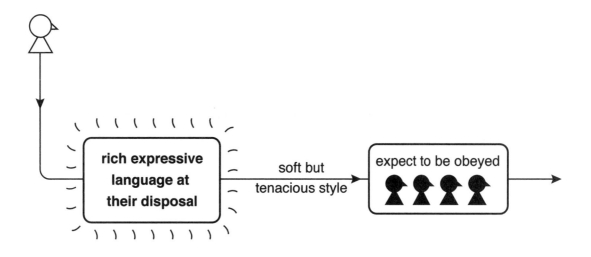

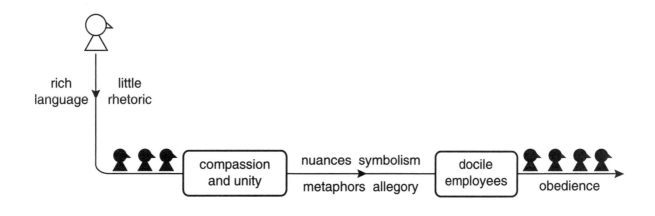

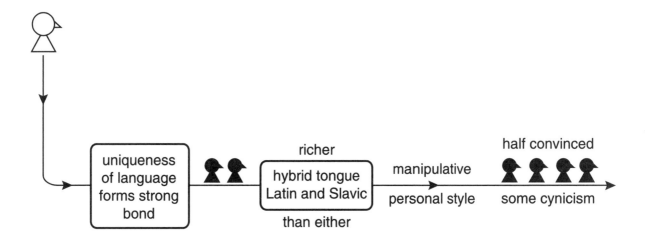

Serbia & Montenegro

The rhetorical use of Serbo-Croat is the vital tool whereby managers mould staff behaviour. Words count more than deeds – the language itself possesses Slavic richness and vitality. In spirit it is persuasive, manipulative and, with the right speaker, effectively coercive. Subordinates are not, however, noted for their docility.

Slovenia

The Slovenian language differs considerably from Serbo-Croat. Slovenians welcome the difference. Both languages possess rich Slavic vocabularies, but whereas Serbs in particular address their followers with frequently fiery rhetoric, Slovenian managers tone down emotion and substitute logic and reasoning.

Croatia

Croatians are proud of the richness of their Slavic tongue and wield it effectively to manage staff and followers. Zagreb and the Dalmatian coast have different dialects. Overall there is a general respect for linguistic fluency and correctness. This, combined with a high level of education, facilitates motivation through elegant discourse.

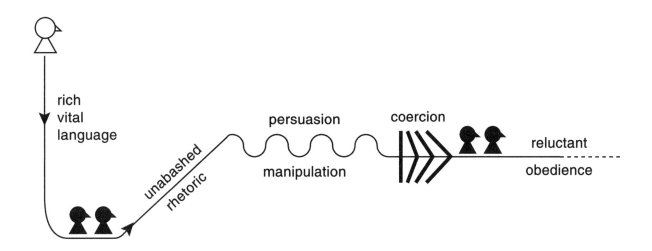

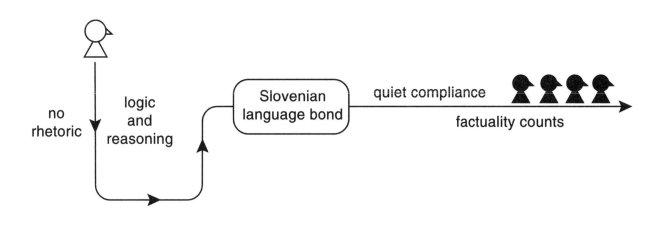

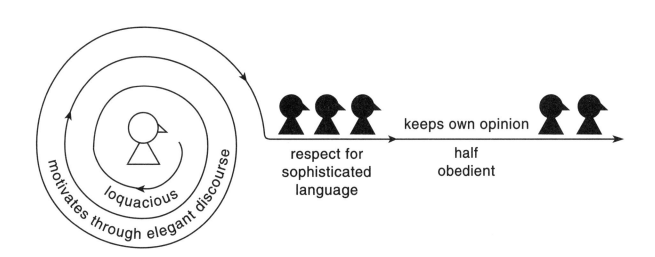

Russia

Nigel Holden sees Russian, where social distance is encoded in highly subtle ways, as resembling Japanese as a flexible management language in network mode. Soviet managers were involved little in such areas as leadership or motivation of employees. The management style utilised threats and coercion to produce results demanded by socialist "planning". Results were disguised (for the better). How Russian will develop as a language of management in the future will depend on modes of address using names and titles and the development of formal and informal mechanisms which do not remind subordinates of coercion and control. Russians respond favourably to a personal, almost conspiratorial, approach.

Ukraine

In Ukraine, staff are managed in different languages – in the East normally in Russian, in the West in Ukrainian. Ukrainian is the state language. It differs from Russian phonetically, lexically and even grammatically, but Russians and Ukrainians can understand each other. The use of Ukrainian in addressing staff is naturally a binding factor. Managers in both parts of Ukraine motivate staff in speech which has elements of emotion, fluency and vibrancy.

Belarus

Belarus is not settled linguistically, and sporadically tries to establish a more defined national identity through the use of the Belarusian language or related media, but business people often have to have recourse to Russian, which has served business purposes since the 1920s. Managers generally adopt an autocratic tone in the bigger urban centres, though they are more "folksy" in the rural areas.

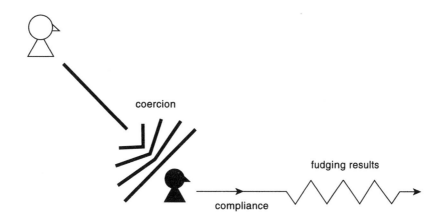

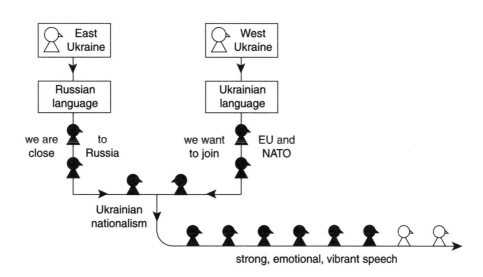

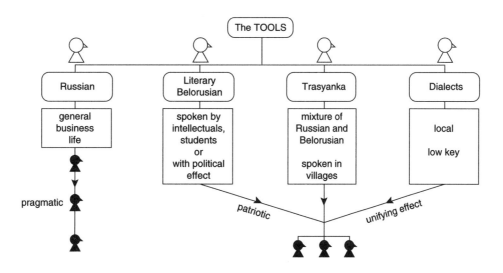

Turkey

Turkish managers are strong and decisive when dealing with their own people. Turkish is spoken forcefully, often in animated tones, and is very much an instrument of persuasion. It also serves as a useful *lingua franca* when dealing with people from Azerbaijan, Uzbekistan, Kazakhstan, Turkmenistan and Kyrgyzstan.

Iran

The language of management in today's Iran varies greatly according to which category the leader or manager belongs to. Religious leaders speak in an authoritarian manner, are moralistic, but attempt to appear just. A large professional managerial class addresses staff in a much more pragmatic manner, albeit often long-winded. They offer help where needed, have bottom line focus and give staff members as much freedom as possible to prosper. Iranian managers who have been educated in the West are generally efficient, punctual and willing to share risks and profits in order to motivate. All classes of leaders pay tribute to the past glories and integrity of the Persian heritage.

Israel

The revival of the Hebrew language as a living, spoken tongue has great significance for Israelis. The alternatives would have been Arabic, English or a linguistic Tower of Babel similar to that in India. Hebrew has the strength of imagery and poetry that exists in Arabic and can inspire staff by its vitality. On top of that, it is a national tongue which binds the speaker and audience in understanding and compliance.

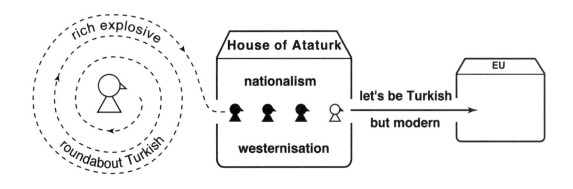

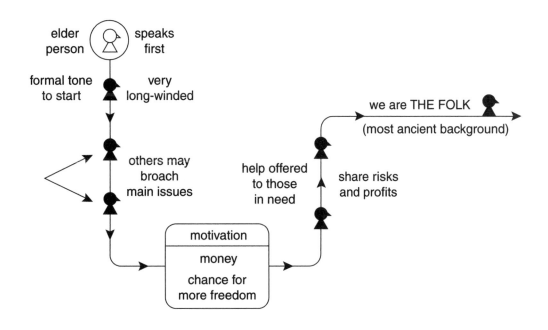

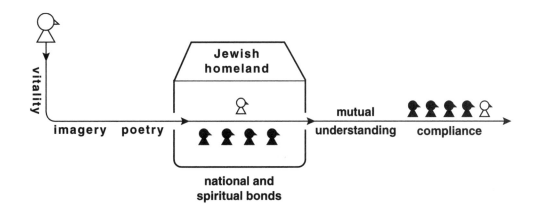

combines modernity with tradition

Iraq

It is difficult to define language of management in today's Iraq. Many commercial managers are dictated to either by their Shiite or Sunni colleagues, and clerics in general dominate the way staff are addressed and handled. Rhetoric is currently at a premium. The language used will make frequent references to Allah and align itself with the precepts and style of the Koran. The inherent rhetorical qualities of the Arabic language lend themselves to reinforcing the speaker's sincerity. A raised voice may be a sign of anger or frustration, but also of genuine feeling and exhortation.

Egypt

In Egypt a good manager is heir to many ancient Egyptian traditions. Arabic, with its Islamic trappings, is of course the language of management. Egyptians consider their version of Arabic the correct one and managers use it with the confidence born of thousands of years of history. Egypt has more speakers of Arabic than any other country. Their long contact with other nationalities (especially the British) allows managers to hint at international experience and cosmopolitanism.

Arab countries (in general)

In the Gulf States a good manager is a good Muslim. The language used will make frequent references to Allah and align itself with the precepts and style of the Koran. A didactic management style is the result. The inherent rhetorical qualities of the Arabic language lend themselves to reinforcing the speaker's sincerity. A raised voice is a sign not of anger, but of genuine feeling and exhortation. The lack of unity among many Arab states gives rise to a great variety of manipulative tactics and strategies.

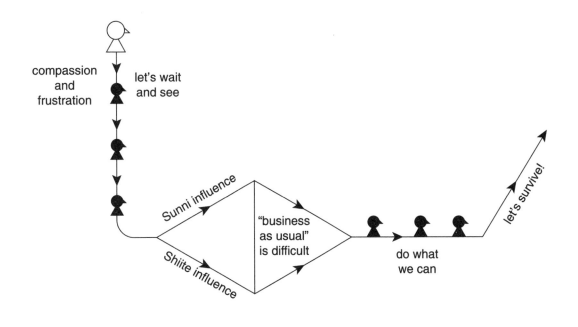

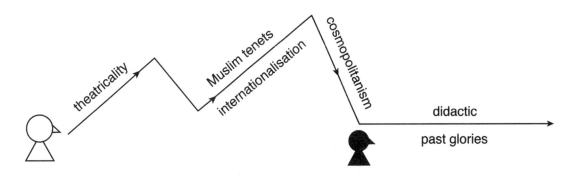

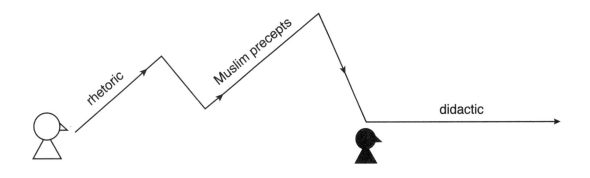

Central Asia
Azerbaijan, Kazakhstan, Uzbekistan, Kyrgyzstan, Tajikistan, Turkmenistan

The language of management varies according to linguistic roots and the identity of people who lead. Tajiks, speaking Indo-European, are apart, and are addressed in terms which encourage morality and kinship rapprochement with 1 million Tajiks living in Afghanistan and even with the Shia Iranians. Moralist doctrine is high on the list of priorities in Turkmenistan and Uzbekistan, though in the latter they let little stand in the way of doing business. Kazakh leaders preach a more relaxed form of Islam than the others and their close oil-related involvement with foreigners (including Westerners) has encouraged pragmatism and a more international outlook. The same applies to Azerbaijan. The basic Turkic element in the cultural group enables five of the nationalities to respond to a management language which is forceful, energetic and unifying, even across national borders.

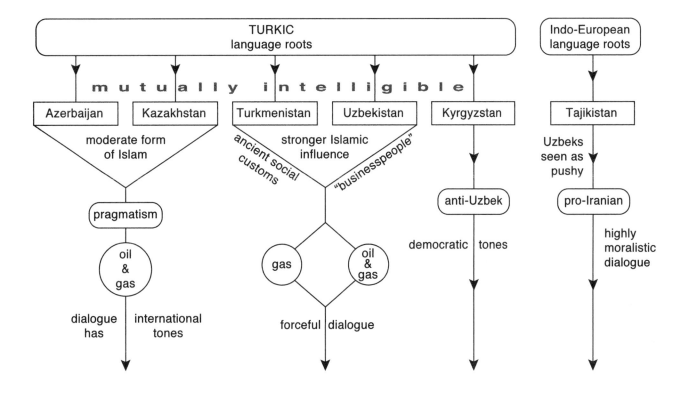

India

The language of management in India is spoken in many tongues, though at higher levels it is often English. The characteristics of Indian English reflect Indian psychology, so that when Hindi, Urdu, Bengali, etc., are used, there will be many commonalities in the approach. Indian English is old-fashioned, flowery and verbose. It is essentially a human, sympathetic language showing respect and often humility to the listener. It is generous in praise, yet reluctant to criticise, since failure in Indian business may quickly be attributed to bad karma. Indian English excels in ambiguity and such things as truth and appearances are often subject to negotiation. Above all, the language of the Indian manager emphasizes the collective nature of the task and challenge. India is far from being a classless society, but the groups will often stand or fall together in the hard world of the sub-continent.

Pakistan

Managers in Pakistan address their staff in several tongues, though at higher levels it is often English or Urdu. The English spoken in Pakistan is, as in India, old-fashioned, flowery and verbose. It is essentially a human, sympathetic language showing respect and, when appropriate, humility to the listener. Urdu is more fiery and coercive than Hindi. Such things as truth and appearances are often subject to negotiation. Above all, the language of the Pakistani manager emphasises the collective nature of the task and Islamic solidarity.

Bangladesh

The language of management in Bangladesh is in Bengali or in English, or occasionally Urdu. Flowery English follows the pattern of eloquent Bengali and staff are motivated by elegant discourse and absence of confrontation. Orders are given in an indirect manner. Westerners may find the style does not lend itself to clarity, but Bangladeshis are skilful in deciphering the intent and wishes of their managers. Politeness and respect counterbalance frankness in manager-staff relations. Foreigners must learn to read between the lines. Staff compliance is the rule rather than the exception.

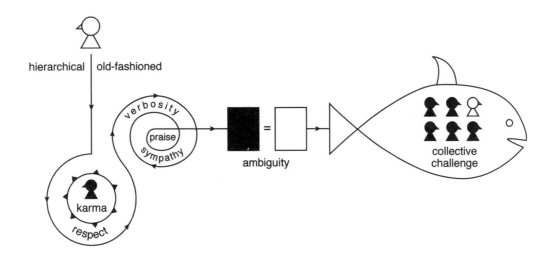

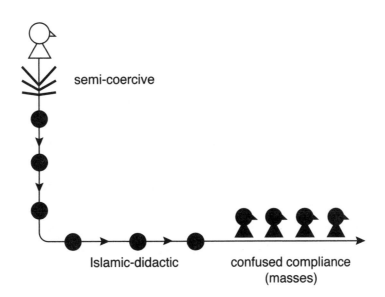

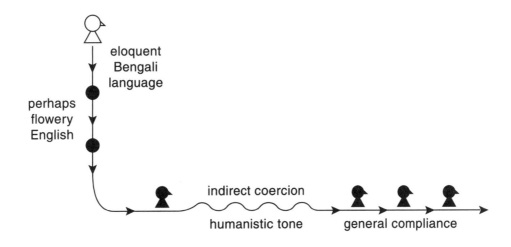

Japan

Japanese managers rarely issue clear orders: they only hint at what has to be done. Instructions often begin with "Sorry to trouble you...". The language is custom-made for this. The structure, which normally stacks up a line of subordinate clauses before the main one, invariably lists the justifications for the directive before it reaches the listener. "Complete September's final report by 5:30" comes out in Japanese as: "It's 10 October today, isn't it? Our controller hasn't asked to see September's report yet. I wonder if he'll pop round tomorrow. You never know with him…" The actual order is never given – there is no need, the staff are already scrambling to their books.

China

There are many varieties of Chinese, though Mandarin (Putonghua) is in gradual ascendancy. Cantonese, and Shanghainese are, however, likely to retain their importance as languages of commerce. Mandarin sounds authoritative to many Chinese and commands obedience. Chinese managers rely heavily on Confucian precepts, which support their authority to no small degree. Their language implies the five unequal relationships as taken for granted; it is delivered softly, implying Confucian standards of wisdom, kindness, moderation and frugality. Like most Asian tongues, it thrives on a certain ambiguity. Politeness and courtesy are mandatory. Subordinates are invariably wooed by this linguistic style.

Hong Kong

The language of management in Hong Kong is basically Cantonese. Differing sharply from Mandarin, it still contains the primary softening elements of Confucian-rules Chinese, but is essentially a language of commerce and is consequently faster, blunter and more factual than most Chinese dialects, with an ever-present sense of urgency and tenacious opposition to any form of red tape. The Cantonese dialect is a unifying factor for all its (numerous) speakers, but especially in Hong Kong.

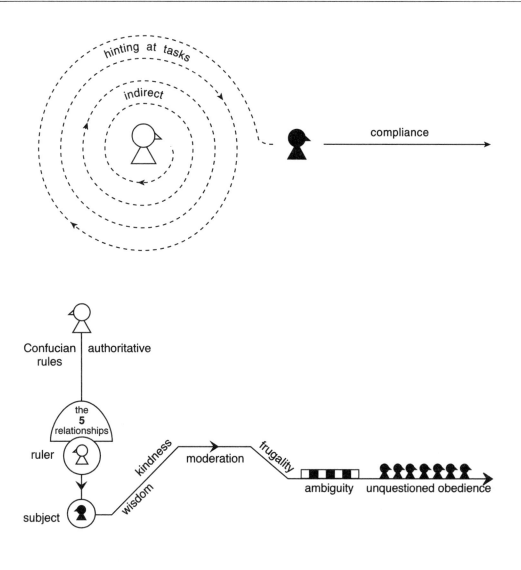

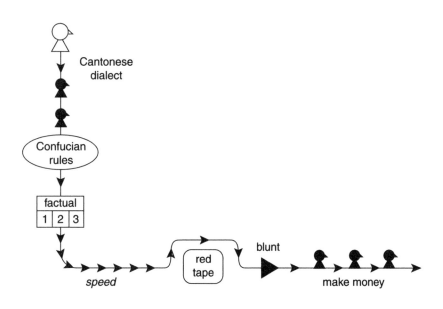

South Korea

Compared to Japanese (to which it is related) the Korean language is less vague and is wielded more forcefully in a somewhat guttural manner. This suits the authoritarian directness of tough Korean managers who beat about the bush much less than Japanese or Chinese. "Kibun" (face), however, must be protected.

North Korea

All management, commercial or political, is subject to Juche doctrine which implacably refuses to entertain or accept any ideas of Western (or even South Korean or Japanese) methods of managing staff. Loyalty is therefore 100% in response to a coercive imposition of "rules of engagement" either in business or socio-political discourse. Korean staff and workers bow to the rules, work one day a week free for the state (often in the fields) and emerge sun-tanned, but entirely passive vis-à-vis their "managers".

The Philippines

Most Filipino managers (and their staff) are fluent both in Tagalog and English. Marcos, when speaking on television or in public, often used to switch from one to the other. A large majority of Filipino staff understand and speak (excellent) English – of the American variety.

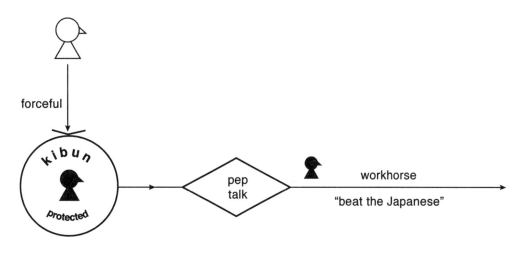

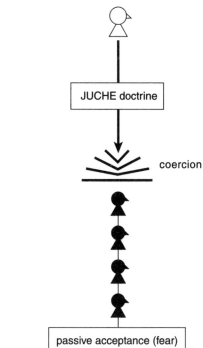

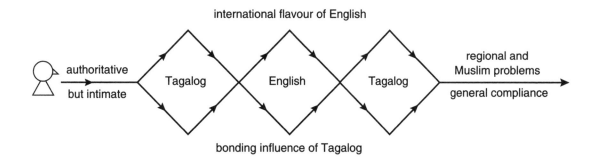

Thailand

The language of Thai managers and other leaders is influenced considerably by the tenets of the Buddhist religion. The concepts of "right speech" and "right understanding" must be observed, as is the necessity of "seeking the truth". Language is therefore gentle, didactic and subtly moralistic. There are many respect forms (more than in most other languages) and these are widely observed. Leaders are expected to be kind to subordinates and will command their loyalty by taking into consideration their needs and desires.

Vietnam

Vietnam is one of the few remaining communist countries in the world and leaders adhere closely to socialist themes, which affects management style. The Vietnamese language is a very rich one, with great literary traditions, so that a little "poetry" creeps in, even in exhortations which are politically influenced. Vietnamese also learned much about oratory from the French, therefore they are strong on logic as well as on Asian intuition.

Myanmar

The managers (generals and stooges) manage staff with a combination of hard-line socialism and freedom of worship (where 75-80% are Theravada Buddhists anyway). People are exhorted to "live the Right Way" – the deprivations suffered in this life will be compensated for in the next one. Ruthless generals enjoy benign photo opportunities in front of temples, in the same way that some Western politicians are eager to align themselves with enthusiastic Christianity.

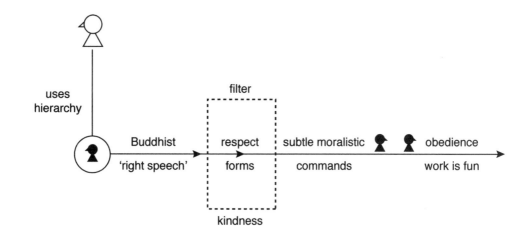

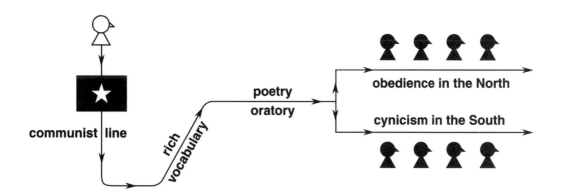

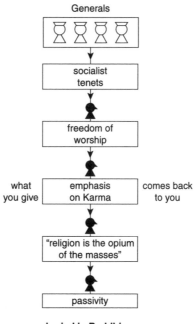

buried in Buddhism

Singapore

Most Singaporeans are managed in Mandarin Chinese. Singaporean managers rely heavily on Confucian precepts, which support their authority to no small degree. Their language implies the five unequal relationships as taken for granted; it is delivered softly, implying Confucian standards of wisdom, kindness, moderation and frugality. Like most Asian tongues, it thrives on a certain ambiguity. Politeness and courtesy are mandatory. Subordinates are invariably wooed by this linguistic style, which also affects Singaporean English (Singlish).

Indonesia

The Indonesian national language – Bahasa – is an artificial construct, being an adaptation of nearby Malay. As there are hundreds of different dialects spoken throughout the Indonesian islands, the government needed a national medium to achieve some kind of linguistic unity. All Indonesians therefore speak at least two languages. Bahasa is essentially a respect language which avoids giving offence to others and has constructions which protect face: oblique forms of criticism, ritualistic utterances, etc. Indonesian managers motivate staff with such softnesses. Because of the military influence, there are also, however, nuances stressing the necessity for unity and occasionally implications of coercion. Chinese managers, who conduct a lot of business, speak Bahasa fluently. Many of them were born in Indonesia.

Malaysia

Malay has many of the characteristics of its Polynesian cousins. It is essentially a respect language which avoids giving offence to others and has constructions which protect face, oblique forms of criticism, ritualistic utterances, etc. Managers motivate staff with such softnesses. Chinese managers, who conduct a lot of business, speak Malay fluently. Many of them were born in Malaysia. English is also frequently used as a language for managing staff. It is closer to British English than American.

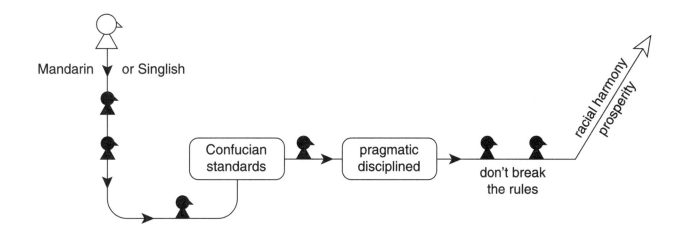

Mandarin or Singlish

Confucian standards → pragmatic disciplined → don't break the rules → racial harmony prosperity

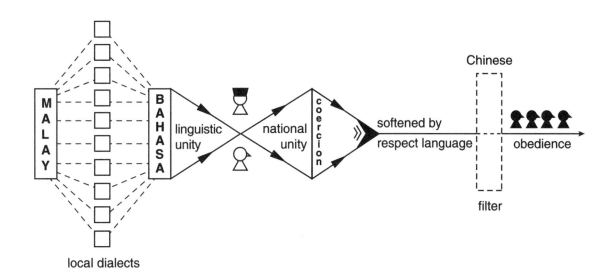

MALAY — BAHASA linguistic unity → national unity → coercion → softened by respect language → Chinese filter → obedience

local dialects

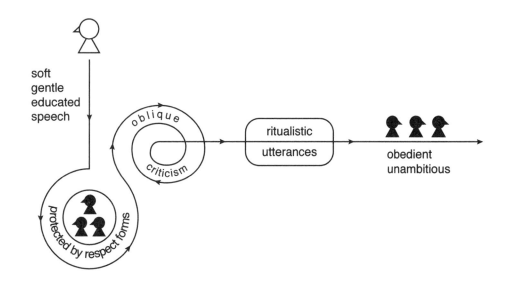

soft gentle educated speech

oblique criticism → ritualistic utterances → obedient unambitious

protected by respect forms

French North Africa

More than half of North Africans are of Berber descent and consequently bilingualism, or trilingualism, is a feature of the regions. Most Algerians and Tunisians speak Berber, Arabic and French, as do the Moroccans, who often can speak Spanish in the north. English is a *lingua franca* for contact with foreigners, though not a language of management. Staff are addressed regularly and at length in language typified by rationality and mild coercion. In view of the high rates of unemployment in the region, staff are generally compliant in accepting orders from superiors. Nationalism often creeps in, especially in Algeria.

Portuguese Africa

Fluency in Portuguese and academic qualifications secured in Portugal facilitate the language of managers in obtaining obedience from their staff. Logic and reasoned argument play a bigger part in Angolan and Mozambican companies than in most other African firms. The argumentative style is closer to that of the francophone countries than that of the former British colonies. Portuguese is a softer language than English or French and diminutives facilitate intimacy of style in general.

Sub-Saharan Africa

The thousand and more tongues of sub-Saharan Africa vary in their linguistic qualities of persuasion and rhetoric, but one can assume that the general African powers of oratory, symbolism and ability to call on the influence of ancestors, constitute an efficient tool for managing and instructing African audiences. Traditional sense of tribal solidarity fortifies the African tendency to follow the collective direction.

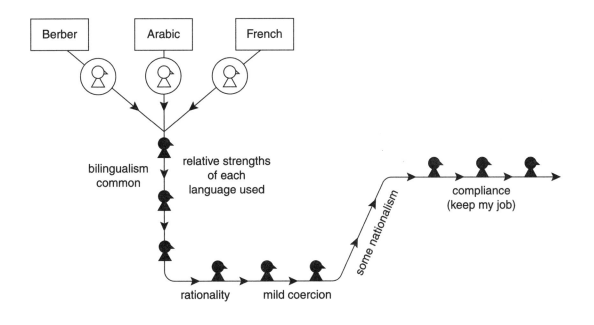

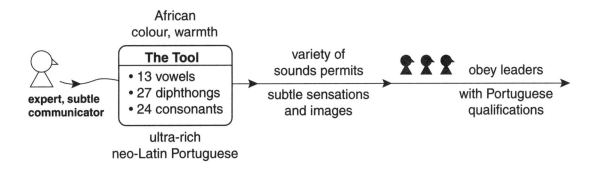

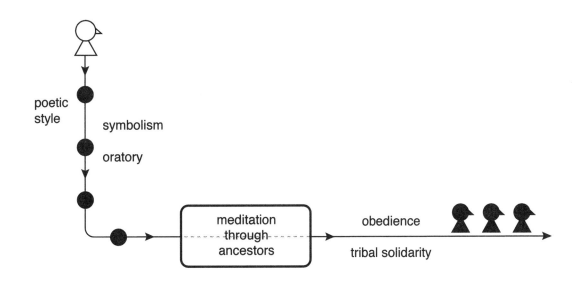

South Africa (black)

Black South Africans, inspired by Nelson Mandela, are rapidly honing their skills in modern political and business oratory, drawing on traditional African strengths such as poetic symbolism and tribal principles. The language of management may be conducted in one or two African languages, but is increasingly in South African English. A slight local (black) accent serves to endear listeners to speakers. The style is both compassionate and persuasive. The future could be bright...

South Africa (white British)

British South African managers generally speak in a soft, educated style, with good vocabulary and articulation. They are skilful persuaders and excel in the soft sell. Understatement is common, as are various kinds of humour, including gentle irony.

South Africa (white Dutch)

Afrikaner leaders address their staff with familiarity, bluntness and heartiness. Their relative isolation as a cultural group enhances their sense of history; their memories of 19th century Afrikaner heroism and endurance is a binding factor. More than the British, they retain a sense of command when dealing with black South Africans, but the attitude is one of bonhomie rather than superiority.

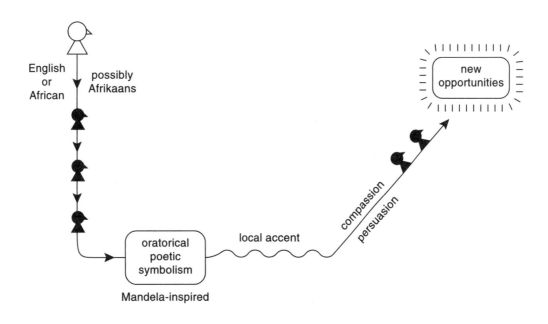

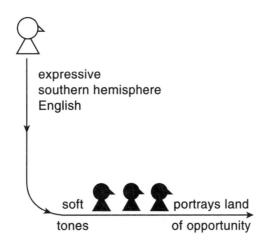

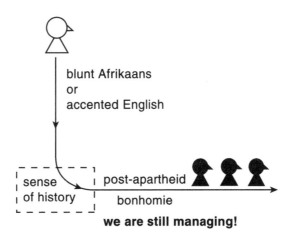

Australia

Australian English is young, vibrant, inventive, humorous, cynical, irreverent, classless, human, original, often teetering between erudite and vulgar – in short a revealing reflection of the "battling" Australian character. As such it is the key to how Australians may be motivated. Australian managers would be ineffective with American pep talk English. (Australians would respond cynically). British or Canadian English, on the other hand, would be too prim or too laid back. The Aussies want their boss to join them in a healthy disrespect for rules and formalism, to lapse into broad speech and cuss a bit, to be affable and ironic at the same time, to avoid flowery or obscure expressions – finally, to call a spade a spade.

New Zealand

New Zealand managers are more conservative, placid and reserved than Australians, whom they see as rather brash and irreverent. By contrast they address their staff in a consistently polite manner and treat women much more sensitively than Australian managers. Team spirit is a New Zealand strong point.

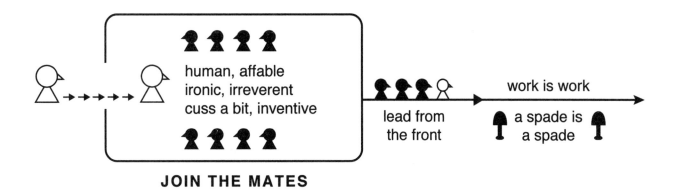

JOIN THE MATES

human, affable
ironic, irreverent
cuss a bit, inventive

lead from
the front

work is work

a spade is
a spade

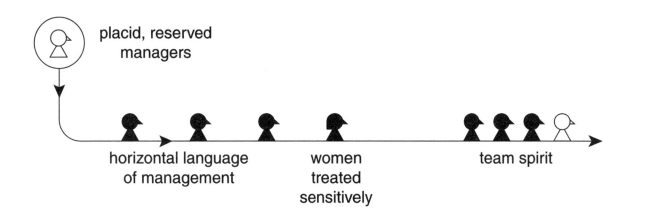

placid, reserved
managers

horizontal language
of management

women
treated
sensitively

team spirit

USA

In the USA the manager, if not always a hero, is viewed in a positive and sympathetic light, as one of the figures responsible for the nation's speedy development and commercial services. The US is a young, vigorous, ebullient nation and its language reflects the national energy and enthusiasm. Americans exaggerate in order to simplify – low-key Britons feel they go "over the top", but the dynamic cliché wears well in the United States The frequent tendency to hyperbolise, exaggerating chances of success, overstating aims or targets, etc., allows American managers to "pump up" their subordinates – to drive them on to longer hours and speedier results. American salespeople do not resist this approach, for they are used to the "hard sell" themselves. Tough talk, quips, wisecracks, barbed repartee – all available in good supply in American English – help them on their way.

Canada

Canadian speech is Americanized British English or muted Anglicized American, depending on which way you look at it. It is low-key, humorous and pleasing and is an excellent tool for motivating laid-back, calm, modest, tolerant staff. Canadian managers will avoid the vague stuffiness of some of their English counterparts, but they will be even more careful to shun American pushiness, hard sell or over-simplification.

Mexico

Mexican Spanish is one of the most melodious and attractive versions of the Iberian languages and is wielded by great skill by Mexican managers addressing their staff. The use of diminutives and other softening devices give the impression of lurking affection and a sense of caring. Tough Castilian, with its extroverted impetus of exuberance, is mitigated by subtle Indian influences of long-standing tradition such as quiet calm, stoicism and understanding of human suffering.

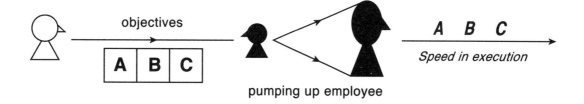

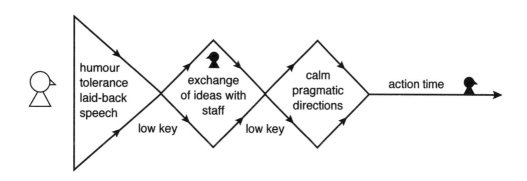

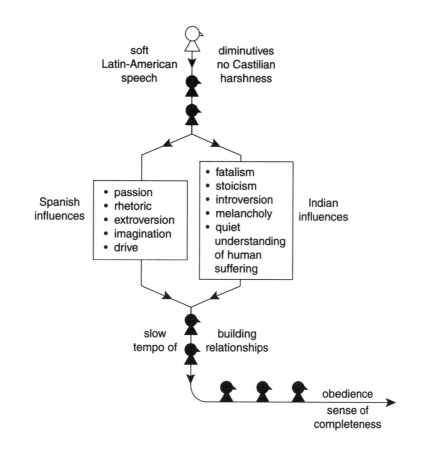

Hispanic America (in general)

The varieties of Spanish spoken in Latin America, from Mexico to Tierra del Fuego, differ considerably in accent and vocabulary according to the region, but they all have a common thread which distinguishes them clearly from Castilian Spanish – they are softer and gentler than the tongue of Castile, using a greater number of diminutives and avoiding the forceful "j" and "ll" sounds of central Spain as well as the ubiquitous lisp (c) of the Spanish court. The language of management of Castilian bosses is declamatory, strident, often harsh and usually irreversible. That of their Latin American counterparts tends to soften the delivery and the message, conveying in the gentleness of the language forms the compassionate style of an Amerindian-influenced continent which understands and accompanies human problems and suffering. Declamation and rhetoric are still present, but a subtle search for agreement and approval can be detected in a certain muting of tone and sound.

Brazil

There is a parallel difference between Brazilian and European Portuguese on the one hand and Latin American Spanish and Castilian on the other. Brazilians, like Latin Americans, avoid the harsher sounds of European Portuguese, employ more diminutives and forms of endearment and generally use the language with more exuberance and abandon than their Iberian cousins. The language as such is an admirable tool for the Brazilian manager addressing staff, who are very concerned with cosiness and cheerfulness, freedom of expression and extroversion, and sometimes racial harmony. Brazilian Portuguese revels in democratic forms, facility of delivery and avoidance of stiffness and formality.

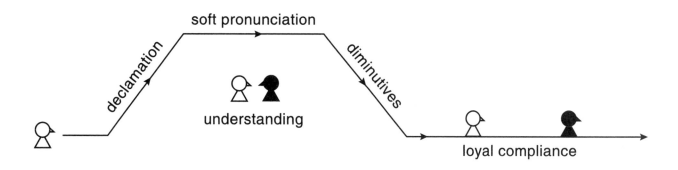

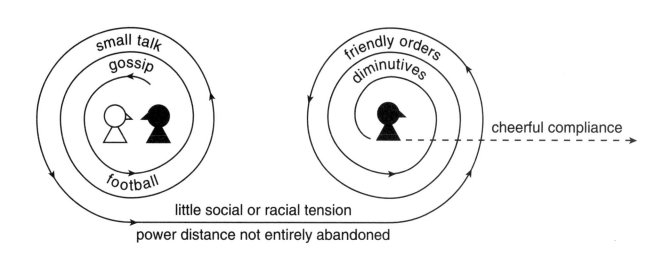

Cuba

Fidel Castro and his brother have succeeded in implanting the Cuban version of Communist doctrine into the minds of all Cubans while at the same time cultivating patriotism. Many Cubans wish for and would derive obvious benefits from a rapprochement with the West, but managers are reluctant to initiate steps which might contravene national harmony or prestige.

Jamaica

Jamaican managers speak kindly and in a folksy manner to their staff, who are very conscious of workers' rights and who voice immediate disapproval if these are in any way infringed. Bosses have to "tread softly" and are in fact quite adept at doing this. Jamaican dialects are a binding factor and the cultural habit of meaningful interaction helps smoothness of management when entered into with sincerity.

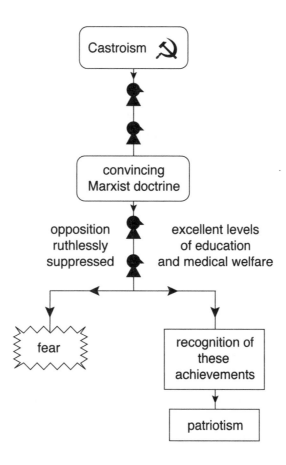

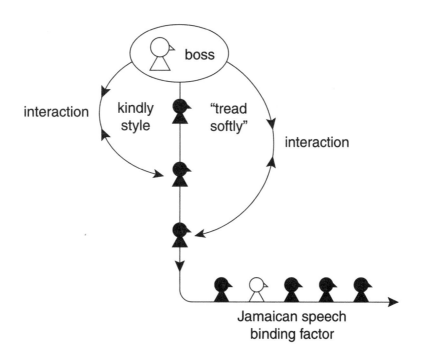

Exercises

1 | **What is your language of management? How do you address your subordinates? Describe it briefly in words below:**

-
-
-
-
-
-

2 | **Now draw a diagram to describe your language of management style in the space below, combining words and visuals:**

3 Flick through the language of management diagrams on pages 195-247. Which cultures are you most similar to and which ones do you differ from? Write them down below:

Similar

Different

-
-
-
-
-

-
-
-
-
-

4 Draw a diagram in the space below (combining words and visuals) to describe the language of management of one of your managers:

5 Visit **www.cultureactive.com** to see National Cultural Profiles on over 80 cultures. Compare and contrast different styles of management language from around the world, as well as many other aspects of social and business communication.

Affective Communication

The aim of this book has been to indicate, in relatively simple diagrammatic form, the great variety in communication patterns which are prevalent in local and international discourse. We have shown how communication is a two-way process, in which the receptivity and attitudes of the listener can affect the meaning of content. We have also indicated how different concepts of leadership, hierarchical constraints and varying psychological approaches in addressing colleagues can enhance, influence or distort messages as they fly from one person to another.

In this final section of the book, we list various communication gambits which could be described as affective or manipulative. Although this type of communication seeks to influence the recipient by applying its own strategies and for its own purposes, we need not consider it as particularly negative. It is, in fact, generally well-meaning, as it is often used to avoid upsetting or embarrassing one's interlocutor. The main intent of English coded speech is to avoid direct criticism of one's partner or colleague by eschewing remarks which might "rock the boat". The same applies to coded speech in meetings where international conventions or considerations of protocol prohibit over-directness or open criticism, particularly in meetings between diplomats or at EU gatherings.

The Americans, particularly, have developed high sensitivity as to what is politically or socially acceptable or unacceptable; the section on politically correct speech gives up-to-date examples for avoiding embarrassment to a variety of underprivileged or in other ways disadvantaged members of society. "Getting to the point" shows how linear-active, multi-active and reactive cultures place different emphases on frankness and delicacy in raising controversial issues, while the sections on understatement, disagreement and euphemisms show different ways of avoiding hyperbole, discord or denigration. The pages dealing with high and low context speech are important in that they point out the danger of reading too much or too little in the statements of one's interlocutor.

The lists of Americanisms and consultant-speak (jargon) are not particularly affective, but are included to familiarise the reader with some expressions which enjoy currency in the Western hemisphere. They should be noted, but not necessarily used.

Finally we include advice with some Golden Rules as to how one should best communicate with the different cultural categories.

The appendix gives examples of affective speech only as it applies to the English language. Different forms and nuances of coded and politically correct speech exist also in other languages and cultures. French people, for example, are careful to avoid upsetting their compatriots in French and tailor their speech accordingly; Spaniards, Italians and Greeks are noted for their delicacy of expression in their own languages. It is English, however, with its dominance in international discourse and communication, which has acquired, through its world-wide use as a *lingua franca*, the power to influence multinational meetings and audiences and to create occasions of misunderstanding among non-English speakers. Hopefully this appendix section will clear up many cases of miscomprehension.

Coded speech

Britons often use coded speech in international teams without being fully aware that they are doing so. This type of parlance – often vague, understated, humorous or coded – can easily be misunderstood by non-English speakers, especially those who tend to take everything literally. Britons rarely say exactly what they mean; they like to leave the interpretation of their remark to the listener, who is supposed to spot nuances, irony, slight changes in the tone of voice. Anything "woolly" or very indirect will usually have a "second" meaning, unclear to the foreigner, but obvious to most Brits.

It is not easy to fall into this way of speaking unless one has lived in the British Isles for at least several months, maybe years. The examples on the page opposite can, however, give a short-cut to some of the more usual expressions and to the hidden agendas behind them.

A Norwegian lady working in the UK for the World Bank found it hard to decode British ways of criticising, praising, suggesting, condemning and abandoning. Understatement and irony often led to the opposite being said to what was actually meant. She also noticed that different British groups used different coding systems. Different types of humour and critique were used according to status and social class.

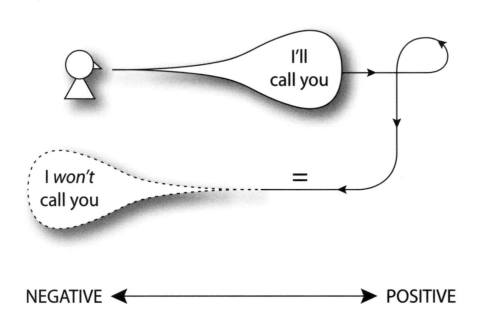

NEGATIVE ⟵————————⟶ POSITIVE

What is said	What is meant
• Hm…interesting idea	Forget it
• We must have a meeting about your idea	Forget it
• We shall certainly consider it	We won't do it
• I'll call you	I won't call you
• That's one way of putting it	What a stupid analysis
• You could say that	I wouldn't
• I agree, up to a point	I disagree
• Correct me if I'm wrong…	I'm right, so don't contradict me
• There is some merit in that	I can't reject it outright
• Could I have a word?	You had better listen to this
• I don't want to make an issue of this	You had better fix it
• It's not for me to influence you either way	This is what I strongly advise you to do
• Let me play the devil's advocate	You've got to see how stupid you are being
• I hear what you say	But I don't agree
• May I make a suggestion?	This is what we are going to do

Coded speech at international meetings

The *lingua franca* at most international meetings (EU committees, GATT Round, Davos and various summits, etc.) is usually English. This gives English-speaking delegates a clear advantage during the discussions. While Americans and Australians excel at direct communication ("tell it how it is"), Britons tend to use a particular form of coded speech born of long political experience in controlling meetings in the days of Empire. They use well-tried, formal but subtle expressions which disguise intent to attack or confront and make it difficult for others to challenge their correctness or abuse of protocol. Non-English speakers are obliged to familiarise themselves with these gambits and often have to use some themselves in order to neutralise the British advantage.

"I shall endeavour to be very brief."

- Mr Chairman, you will surely agree…

  Watch your step, Mr Chairman!

- With respect, Mr Chairman…

  I am going to be disrespectful

- With the greatest possible respect, Mr Chairman…

  I am going to be extremely disrespectful

- I shall be very brief

  I am going to speak for about 20 minutes

- I shall endeavour to be very brief

  I intend to speak for more than 20 minutes

- While I have the floor…

  I intend to make sure no-one else has it

- While I have some sympathy for my colleague's remarks…   He's talking rubbish

- I do not wish to stand in the way…

  But I am going to

- Speaking off the cuff

  Using a prepared text, but not admitting it

- If I have understood correctly…

  I am going to distort what you have just said

- I haven't had time to study the document in depth

  I haven't even opened it

- Please remind me once again your strategy

  I haven't been paying the slightest of attention

Politically correct speech

A feature of modern American speech is their preoccupation with what is or is not politically correct. The preoccupation derives from the litigious nature of US society where avoidance of sexual or racial discrimination has widened to include any type of disadvantaged individual. For instance, it is no longer permissible in American social or business circles to say "negro", "red Indian", "stupid" or "fat", particularly in the presence of the person concerned. It is hardly likely that European or Asian colleagues could master the following selection of preferred expressions, but it is advisable to be familiar with some of them.

Vertically challenged

Horizontally challenged

- Native Americans
- First Nations   } Red Indians
- Indigenous peoples

- Inuit   Eskimos

- Afro-Americans   Negroes

- Asian-Americans   Orientals

- Chicanos   Mexicans

- Cow hunters   Cowboys

- Heavily-pigmented   dark-skinned

- Person of substance   fat

- Horizontally challenged   fat

- Vertically challenged   short

- Uncompromising natural aroma   body odour

- Cosmetically attractive   good-looking

- Differently visaged   ugly

- Ethically disoriented   criminal

- Non-traditional shopper   shoplifter

- Client of the correctional system   convict

- Physically inconvenienced   disabled, cripple

- Underprivileged   poor

- Fiscal under-achievers   poor

- Emotionally different   mad

Understatement

Understatement is an essentially British form of coded speech which minimises or lessens the value or quality or something or somebody. A famous literary figure once described it as "the supreme virtue of the Englishman." It is the art of stating something with restraint, especially for greater effect. It may indicate modesty: "I'm pretty much a beginner at this"; or praise: "I've seen worse reports". The use of understatement seeks to avoid over-emphasis or exaggeration and is a kind of antidote to American hype. It delivers less than the truth "I think it might do" (= it's excellent). It involves an intentional lack of emphasis in expression as in irony: "I think I've got the message" (= you don't have to tell me 10 times).

Understatement has a sister-construction, LITOTES, as in "He is no coward" (= he is very brave) or "she isn't the ugliest woman I've ever met" (= she is very beautiful).

In business, understatement is often used by English, Canadian, Finnish, Swedish, Chinese and Japanese executives, who prefer low-key dialogue to rhetorical exchanges.

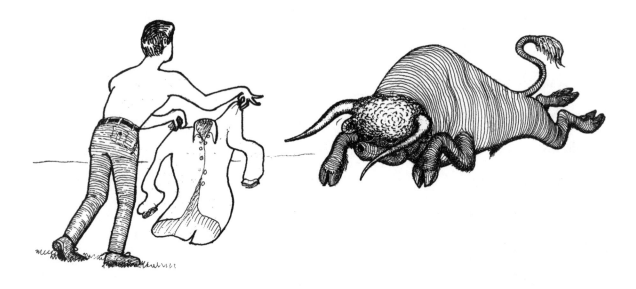

"He's no coward."

- It's not bad
- I've seen worse
- I've seen better
- He can play a bit (Pele)
- I think it'll do the job
- That might just be a bit tricky
- It's not on
- I'm not quite with you on that one
- It's a bit thick
- The Board might take a dim view of that
- He frequently underachieves
- I suppose I could be seen with you
- Average
- Jack's finally managed to sell something

It's excellent

It's very good

It was dreadful

He's a great player

It's exactly what you need

It's impossible

It's disgraceful

It's totally unacceptable

It's disgraceful

They'll crucify you

He's useless

You look absolutely ravishing

Fantastic shot! (tennis)

Jack's sales are incredibly good this month

Euphemisms

Euphemisms constitute a particular form of coded speech, where one substitutes an agreeable word or expression for one which might offend. It comes from a Greek word meaning "to speak favourably". One can have a positive or negative view of euphemisms depending on the degree to which they are used or indeed one's own social class. Positive definitions include discretion in speech: lower end of the achievement range = unsuccessful; refinement of language: pass away, join the great majority = die; softening of expression: tipsy, merry = drunk. Negative definitions include exaggerated genteelism: powder one's nose, wash one's hands = go to the toilet; over-delicate words: charlady = charwoman, professor = teacher, engineer = mechanic; less than truthful language: developing countries = backward; friendly fire = shoot your own troops. Weekley spoke of euphemisms as "that form of speech which avoids calling things by their names". For instance all that relates to sex is heavily veiled: in an interesting condition = pregnant; private parts = sexual organs. There exist also certain religious interdictions: one must be careful when speaking of God. This gives rise to expression such as "by gad!" (God) and "gee-whizz!" (Jesus). The polar counterparts of euphemisms are obscenities (defecate = shit).

Although the (southern) English are the champions of coded speech, Americans tend to euphemise more than the British, probably due to their concern with politically correct speech. Some US examples are: friendly fire; let go = sack; pre-owned cars = second hand; take out = kill, murder.

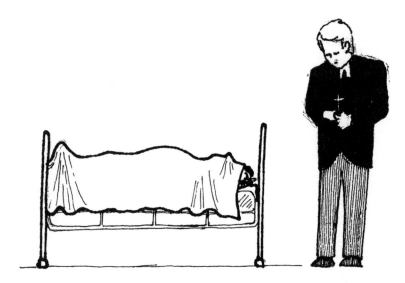

Negative patient-care outcome

- Charlady   charwoman

- Low-cost housing   slums

- Friendly fire   shot by your own troops

- Negative patient–care outcome   death in hospital

- She certainly communicates well   she gossips

- He has a strong oral culture   he can't read or write

- We'll have to review your position   you're going to be fired

- Remuneration must inevitably be results-oriented   you are coming off the payroll

- It has lots of future potential   it has failed

- She has interpersonal skills   she's computer-illiterate

- Negative cash flow   losses

- Between career changes   unemployed

- Explicit language   obscenities

- Pre-adult   a kid

- Senior citizens
- Golden agers   old people
- Oldsters
- Retirees

Americanisms

American speech is quick, mobile and opportunistic, reflecting the speed and agility of the young country. The wisecrack is basic to their discourse. American humour excels in quips, barbed retorts and repartee, typical of the dog-eat-dog society of early America.

Exaggeration and hyperbole are at the bottom of most American expressions, contrasting sharply with the understated nature of the British. In the early days of pioneering, when immigrants speaking many varieties of halting English were thrown together in simple, often primitive surroundings, plainness and unsophisticated language were at a premium. The well-worn cliché was more understandable than originality or elegance of expression. The American language has never recovered from the exigencies of this period. The ordinary man's speech tends to be "tough talk", rather reminiscent of cowboy parlance or Chicago gangland speech of the 1920s. The nation's obsession with show business and the pervasive influence of Hollywood have accentuated and, to some extent, perpetuated this trend. To make a start is to get the show on the road, to take a risk in a business venture is to fly by the seat of your pants, lawyers are shysters, accountants are bean counters, and, if you have no choice, it's the only game in town.

It's the only game in town

Here are some expressions which are common in the US but often unfamiliar to European ears:

American	British equivalent
He's on a roll	He's doing well
That's a beautiful scenario	We might find a way of making that work
It's the only game in town	I have no other choice
Go for broke	Stake everything on one venture
If they ever come back from the grave	If they are ever a force in business again
I want black ink on the bottom line	We must go for profit
I need it like yesterday	It's urgent
It just won't fly	It isn't viable
I can't fly it by the seat of my pants	I need more information
Don't make waves	Leave well alone
He never got to first base	He never got started
He's out in left field	He's way off the point
We're playing for all the marbles	It's a big deal
This is a whole new ball game	It's a different type of business
If you will play ball	If you co-operate

Gobbledygook (consultant-speak)

The second half of the 20th century saw the rise of a certain type of language which is often referred to as "gobbledygook" or "doublespeak". Used frequently by consultants, it is a form of difficult and pompous jargon wielded by so-called specialists who apparently seek sophistication of expression. Purists are more likely to consider it a misuse or distortion of the English language. The examples on the opposite page are given for the reader's elucidation or amusement, certainly not for imitation!

Head-to-heads

- Delayering, delevelling   firing middle managers

- Downsizing, rightsizing   firing as many people as possible to be able to stay in business

- Marginalising   putting someone aside

- Granting empowerment   giving imaginary powers to lower middle managers

- Business process re-engineering   trying to placate dissatisfied customers

- Negative performance indicators   complaints

- Window in the diary   free time

- Head-to-heads   meetings

- Niche marketeers   specialists

Job description (UK)

"Wanted: a temporary part-time libraries North-west inter-library loan business unit administration assistant."

Cover-up (US)

Former White House Press Secretary, Ron Ziegler, replying to a question about whether some Watergate tapes were still intact:

"I would feel that most of the conversations that took place in those areas of the White House that did have the recording system would in almost their entirety be in existence but the special prosecutor, the court, and, I think, the American people are sufficiently familiar with the recording system to know where the recording devices existed and to know the situation in terms of the recording process but I feel, although the process has not been undertaken yet in preparation of the material to abide by the court decision, really, what the answer to that question is."

Disagreement

There are times in life when we feel we have to disagree with an interlocutor – he or she may be a friend, colleague, superior or opposing negotiator. Expressing disagreement comes more easily to some cultures than to others. Germans disagree openly, considering it to be the most honest way. Americans and Finns are also admirably frank and direct. French people disagree openly, but politely. In the Japanese culture, open disagreement is taboo – indeed most Asians are nervous about it.

British people also dislike open conflict and use various instances of coded speech to soften their opposition in conversation. The examples on the opposite page indicate how ways of expressing disagreement may be affected by Swedish love of consensus, Chinese fondness for ambiguity, Italian indirectness, Belgian compromise, Japanese concern about loss of face, American cynicism, Swiss correctness, Filipino deference to superiors, Brazilian cheerfulness and Finnish humorous reticence.

"Half of us agree."

- I don't agree   German
- I'm afraid I don't share your opinion   French
- I agree, up to a point   British
- Let's agree to disagree   British
- We agree   Japanese
- We agree if all of us agree   Swedish
- Half of us agree   Belgian
- We agree and disagree at the same time   Chinese
- Have another cup of coffee   Finnish
- I agree with you, but I don't think my Board of Directors will   Swiss
- You gotta be kidding   US
- You are the boss   Filipino
- I suppose anything's possible   Brazilian
- Let's go and have a Campari and talk about it tomorrow   Italian
- Why are the lights still on in the kitchen?   Jewish

High and low context

One of the frequent problems of communication among members of an international team is the difference in style between high context and low context speakers (and listeners). Hall (1976) showed how cultures differ in the extent to which personal communication occurs explicitly via spoken words (low context) or implicitly (high context) through the context of particular situations, the relationship itself and physical cues including non-verbal behaviour. High context cultures such as Japanese and French rely on understanding through shared experience and history to give implicit messages, whereas low context Americans feel they have "to spell it all out".

The manager of an international team must also try to calculate how much different people deduce from the utterances of others. A high context Italian will deduce much more from simple American messages than the American realises. The Italian is "reading between the lines" when perhaps he is not meant to!

For example, a sensitive Italian or French person might interpret a somewhat rough American manner of accepting terms as an actual indication of distaste for the terms, whereas the American meant simply what he said, and no more. See upper diagram on the page opposite.

By the same token, an American or Australian, who expects things to be "spelled out", may have a greatly reduced understanding of a Japanese or Mexican utterance highly charged with innuendo and *sous-entendus*.

In the latter case, the high context speaker will assume that the entire message, with all its implications, has been fully understood. For instance, a Japanese may be quite satisfied that the physical cues he released in speaking manner and tone of voice indicated clearly that he is not in favour of a certain procedure, whereas the Australian has probably interpreted the politeness and apparent acquiescence of the Japanese as a sign of agreement. See lower diagram on the page opposite.

A low context American v. a high context Italian

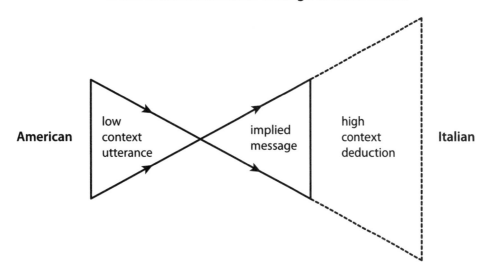

"All right, we'll accept your terms" (spoken brusquely)

A high context Japanese v. a low context Australian

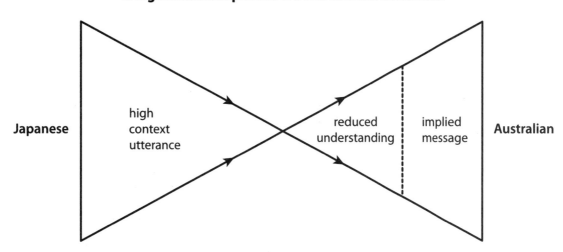

"We'll do our very best to deliver on time"

High and low context advertising

High and low context expression is seen also in the ways different cultures create advertisements.

The French ad below uses only eight words. Implicit, however, is the pleasure experienced by passengers as they enjoy a glass of wine and a delicious selection of French cheeses as they wend their way to Paris!

The German ad opposite, by contrast, is extreme in its explicitness, spelling out in detail the pains taken by the airline to ensure the passengers' safety.

FLAVOUR OF FRANCE.

AIR FRANCE
ASK THE WORLD OF US

A high context advertisement

Choosing Lufthansa quality is choosing experience and responsibility.

When you're used to carrying a lot of responsibilities, you tend to expect the same sense of responsibility from others. Especially when you put yourself in their hands when travelling. And that's exactly why Lufthansa refuses to make a compromise when it comes to perfection. It's why we invest DM 1.1 billion every year in the most uncompromising service and maintenance system. It's why some 11,000 Lufthansa technicians, who spend years being trained in a system that sets worldwide standards, always feel fully responsible for you.

In theory, of course, we could afford to be a little less perfect in our quality measures.

At least, if we were happy just to follow the statutory standards laid down by manufacturers. But we think that's too little to meet the uncompromising quality levels we've set ourselves. Lufthansa was the world's first airline to practise a radical and farsighted technology that checks the health of our engines every second they're in flight. And even at the design and production stages of our aircraft, we leave nothing to chance. On the new 747-400, our technical teams carry out over 1,000 additional checks on top of the manufacturer's own quality control.

To illustrate our quality level in another way: just imagine that behind every second seat on a Lufthansa plane, there's a Lufthansa technician. It's when you realize you have that much perfection behind you that you can really explain the good feeling of flying Lufthansa.

A low context advertisement

Getting to the point

A well-known saying in many countries is: "The shortest distance between two points is a straight line". "Getting to the point" in conversation might well be indicated visually:

This would apply, however, only to linear-active cultures such as German or American.

A person from a multi-active culture (Italy or France) would be less direct. The route would be more indirect, thus:

In a reactive culture (like Japan or China) the route would be far more roundabout. Indeed point B might actually never be reached! Thus:

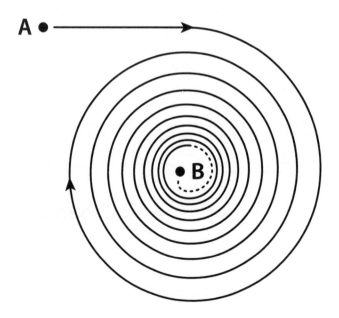

In the US, the message "we can't accept an increase in price" is far more likely to be in Italy "I'll take the increase to our purchasing department and let's see if we can negotiate something". In Japan, the actual refusal would probably not be stated, but the context would be unmistakable. The following is a verbatim extract of a conversation between an American supplier and a Japanese manager during the 1990s recession:

"Ah yes, the price ... *so desu ne* ... as you know, we greatly admire the quality of your product – it has always been the policy of our company to buy best quality, even in difficult times ... *so desu ne* ... Our senior Vice President, Mr Yamamoto, was just saying the other day how much he values the co-operation between our two companies – we have been doing business together for over 20 years, *ne*? We have always chosen to buy your merchandise, even though many of your competitors have approached us many times with cheaper products. Whenever we can, we pay top dollar for valued added services, *ne*?

As you know, Japan is at the moment in severe recession and this has naturally affected our company too; we have had to cut many budgets and, believe it or not, we had to downsize to some extent – most unusual for a Japanese company! It is getting very hard for us to manage our cash flow – many of the Japanese firms we sell to have been very slow in paying us. Even some of them have discontinued their contracts with us; they are, as you say, hard up. Well, we continue to buy the best we can, it's quite a strain on us at times. Mr Suzuki, our Purchasing Manager, was saying only last week that we should make every effort to pay your asking price. He thought it was rather high, but quality is important for him, naturally. Our finance department have other ideas, you know they are always trying to economise – I'm sure you have similar problems in your company. You can rest assured I shall make every effort on your behalf. Mr Yamamoto, as you know, is one of your biggest supporters – it's unfortunate he is seconded to our office in the United States.

Of course there will be some delay before we make a decision; please keep in contact with me if any ideas occur to you. Not that we doubt the validity of your pricing...

By the way Mr Yamamoto much enjoyed being invited by your Senior Vice President Mr Matthews to play golf at Pebble Beach last August. He described it as one of the best moments..."

Golden rules for communicating successfully across cultural categories

The Lewis Model has established three categories of cultural groups:

Linear-active (e.g. Germans), **Multi-active** (e.g. Italians) and **Reactive** (e.g. Japanese). Each of these categories has its own basic style of communication.

Linear-active people tend to be task-oriented, highly organised planners who complete action chains by doing one thing at a time, preferably in accordance with a linear agenda. They prefer straightforward and direct discussion, depending on facts and figures they obtain from reliable, often printed or computer-based sources. Speech is for information exchange, and conversationalists take turns talking and listening. Truthful rather than diplomatic, linear-actives do not fear confrontation, adhering to logic rather than emotions. They partly conceal feelings and value a certain amount of privacy. Results are key, as is moving forward quickly and compromising when necessary to achieve a deal.

Multi-actives are emotional, loquacious and impulsive people; they attach great importance to family, feelings, relationships, and people in general. They set great store by compassion and human warmth. They like to do many things at the same time and are poor followers of agendas. Conversation is roundabout and animated as everyone tries to speak and listen at the same time. Not surprisingly, interruptions are frequent, pauses in conversation few. Multi-actives are uncomfortable with silence and can seldom tolerate it.

In business, relationships and connections are seen as more important than products. The former pave the way for the sale of the latter. Relationships are best when they are face-to-face; they cannot be maintained over a protracted period simply by written correspondence or phone calls. They much prefer to obtain their information directly from people and trade in rumour and gossip. Multi-actives are flexible and frequently change their plans, which in themselves are not as detailed as those of linear-actives. Improvisation and handling chaos are strong points.

In business, their speech is characterised by charisma, rhetoric, manipulation and negotiated truth. They are diplomatic and tactful and often circumvent laws and officialdom to take "short cuts".

Reactives, or listeners, rarely initiate action or discussion, preferring to first listen to and establish the other's position, then react to it and formulate their own opinion. Reactives listen before they leap, concentrating on what the speaker is saying and refusing to let their minds wander (difficult for Latins). Rarely, if ever, do they interrupt a speaker during a discourse/speech/presentation. When the speaker is finished, they do not reply immediately, but rather leave a decent period of silence after the speaker has stopped in order to show respect for the weight of the remarks, which must be considered unhurriedly and with due deference.

Even when representatives of a reactive culture begin their reply, they are unlikely to voice any strong opinion immediately. A more probable tactic is to ask further questions on what has been said in order to clarify the speaker's intent and aspirations. Reactives are introverts, distrustful of a surfeit of words.

In reactive cultures the preferred mode of communication is monologue-pause-reflection-monologue.

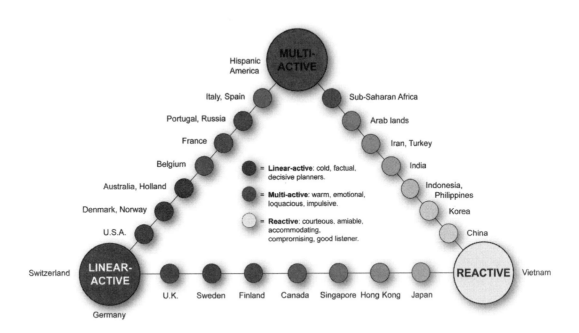

Golden rules for communicating with LINEAR-ACTIVE people

- Speech is for information

- Talk and listen in equal proportions

- Discuss one thing at a time

- Be polite but direct

- Partly conceal feelings

- Use logic and rationality

- Interrupt only rarely

- Stick to facts

- Concentrate on the deal (job)

- Prioritise truth over diplomacy

- Follow rules, regulations, laws

- Maintain word-deed correlation

- Complete action chains

- Stay results-oriented

- Stick to the agenda

- Compromise to achieve deal

- Respect officialdom

- Respect contracts and written word

- Reply quickly to written communication or emails

- Restrain body language

- Look for short-term profit

- Be punctual

Golden rules for communicating with MULTI-ACTIVE people

- Speech is for opinions

- Let them talk at length

- Reply fully

- Be prepared to discuss several things at once

- Be prepared for several people talking at once

- Display feelings and emotion

- Remember people and feelings are more important than facts

- Interrupt when you like

- Truth is flexible and situational

- Be diplomatic rather than direct

- Be gregarious and socialising

- Think aloud

- Complete human transactions

- Digress from agenda and explore interesting ideas

- Seek and give favours with key people

- Remain relationship-oriented

- The spoken word is important

- Contracts may often be renegotiated

- Reputation is as important as profit

- Overt body language and tactility are acceptable

- Accept unpunctuality

Golden rules for communicating with REACTIVE people

- Speech is to promote harmony
- Good listening is important
- Never interrupt
- Never confront
- Never cause anyone to lose face
- Never disagree openly
- Suggestions, especially criticism, must be indirect
- Be ambiguous, so as to leave options open
- Statements are promises
- Prioritise diplomacy over truth
- Follow rules but interpret them flexibly
- Share as much as you can
- Utilise networks
- Talk slowly
- Do things at appropriate times
- Don't rush or pressure them
- Observe fixed power distances and hierarchy
- Show exaggerated respect for older people
- Go over things several times
- Face-to-face contact is important
- Work hard at building trust
- Long term profit is preferable
- Be punctual

Richard Lewis Communications Licensed Partners

In addition to the cultures featured in this book, an extensive library of materials is provided for trainers online. Richard Lewis Communications' (RLC) Licensed Partners have exclusive access to slides using the same visual approach, expanded to 80 cultures, plus additional materials under headings such as team-working, trust, and meeting styles. These high-quality materials are not available anywhere else, and provide trainers with a considerable competitive advantage.

Here is a partial list of the materials available at the time of printing. The library is continually expanded and updated – please visit the website for the latest information.

Communication Patterns
Arab countries, Argentina, Australia, Austria, Bangladesh, Belgium, Belize, Bolivia, Brazil, Bulgaria, Canada, Chile, China, Colombia, Costa Rica, Croatia, Czech Republic, Denmark, Ecuador, Egypt, El Salvador, Estonia, Finland, France, Germany, Greece, Guatemala, Hispanic America, Honduras, Hong Kong, Hungary, India, Indonesia, Iraq, Ireland, Israel, Italy, Japan, Kazakhstan, Korea, Kuwait, Latvia, Lithuania, Malaysia, Mexico, Netherlands, Nicaragua, Nigeria, Norway, Pakistan, Panama, Paraguay, Peru, Philippines, Poland, Portugal, Romania, Russia, Saudi Arabia, Serbia & Montenegro, Singapore, Slovakia, Slovenia, South Africa, Spain, Sub-Saharan Africa, Sweden, Switzerland, Taiwan, Thailand, Tunisia, Turkey, Uganda, United Arab Emirates, United Kingdom, Uruguay, USA, Uzbekistan, Venezuela, Vietnam.

Listening Habits
Arab countries, Argentina, Australia, Austria, Bangladesh, Belgium, Belize, Bolivia, Brazil, Bulgaria, Canada, Chile, China, Colombia, Costa Rica, Croatia, Czech Republic, Denmark, Ecuador, Egypt, El Salvador, Estonia, Finland, France, Germany, Greece, Guatemala, Hispanic America, Honduras, Hong Kong, Hungary, India, Indonesia, Iraq, Ireland, Israel, Italy, Japan, Kazakhstan, Korea, Kuwait, Latvia, Lithuania, Malaysia, Mexico, Netherlands, Nicaragua, Nigeria, Norway, Pakistan, Panama, Paraguay, Peru, Philippines, Poland, Portugal, Romania, Russia, Saudi Arabia, Serbia & Montenegro, Singapore, Slovakia, Slovenia, South Africa, Spain, Sub-Saharan Africa, Sweden, Switzerland, Taiwan, Thailand, Tunisia, Turkey, Uganda, United Arab Emirates, United Kingdom, Uruguay, USA, Uzbekistan, Venezuela, Vietnam.

Audience Expectations
Arab countries, Argentina, Australia, Austria, Bangladesh, Belgium, Belize, Bolivia, Brazil, Bulgaria, Canada, Chile, China, Colombia, Costa Rica, Croatia, Czech Republic, Denmark, Ecuador, Egypt, El Salvador, Estonia, Finland, France, Germany, Greece, Guatemala, Hispanic America, Honduras, Hong Kong, Hungary, India, Indonesia, Iraq, Ireland, Israel, Italy, Japan, Kazakhstan, Korea, Kuwait, Latvia, Lithuania, Malaysia, Mexico, Netherlands, Nicaragua, Nigeria, Norway, Pakistan, Panama, Paraguay, Peru, Philippines, Poland, Portugal, Romania, Russia, Saudi Arabia, Serbia & Montenegro, Singapore, Slovakia, Slovenia, South Africa, Spain, Sub-Saharan Africa, Sweden, Switzerland, Taiwan, Thailand, Tunisia, Turkey, Uganda, United Arab Emirates, United Kingdom, Uruguay, USA, Uzbekistan, Venezuela, Vietnam.

Leadership
Arab countries, Argentina, Australia, Austria, Bangladesh, Belgium, Belize, Bolivia, Brazil, Bulgaria, Canada, Chile, China, Colombia, Costa Rica, Croatia, Czech Republic, Denmark, Ecuador, Egypt, El Salvador, Estonia, Finland, France, Germany, Greece, Guatemala, Hispanic America, Honduras, Hong Kong, Hungary, India, Indonesia, Iraq, Ireland, Israel, Italy, Japan, Kazakhstan, Korea, Kuwait, Latvia, Lithuania, Malaysia, Mexico, Netherlands, Nicaragua, Nigeria, Norway, Pakistan, Panama, Paraguay, Peru, Philippines, Poland, Portugal, Romania, Russia, Saudi Arabia, Serbia & Montenegro, Singapore, Slovakia, Slovenia, South Africa, Spain, Sub-Saharan Africa, Sweden, Switzerland, Taiwan, Thailand, Tunisia, Turkey, Uganda, United Arab Emirates, United Kingdom, Uruguay, USA, Uzbekistan, Venezuela, Vietnam.

Language of Management
Arab countries, Argentina, Australia, Austria, Bangladesh, Belgium, Belize, Bolivia, Brazil, Bulgaria, Canada, Chile, China, Colombia, Costa Rica, Croatia, Czech Republic, Denmark, Ecuador, Egypt, El Salvador, Estonia, Finland, France, Germany, Greece, Guatemala, Hispanic America, Honduras, Hong Kong, Hungary, India, Indonesia, Iraq, Ireland, Israel, Italy, Japan, Kazakhstan, Korea, Kuwait, Latvia, Lithuania, Malaysia, Mexico, Netherlands, Nicaragua, Nigeria, Norway, Pakistan, Panama, Paraguay, Peru, Philippines, Poland, Portugal, Romania, Russia, Saudi Arabia, Serbia & Montenegro, Singapore, Slovakia, Slovenia, South Africa, Spain, Sub-Saharan Africa, Sweden, Switzerland, Taiwan, Thailand, Tunisia, Turkey, Uganda, United Arab Emirates, United Kingdom, Uruguay, USA, Uzbekistan, Venezuela, Vietnam.

Human Mental Programming

Teams: Linear-active Team, Multi-active Team, Reactive Team, Mono-cultural Team, Multi-cultural Team

Meetings: Linear-active Meetings, Multi-active Meetings, Reactive Meetings

Cultural Anchorages: Linear-active, Multi-active, Reactive

CultureActive

National Cultural Profiles – The web-based global cultural database

The National Cultural Profile series is a unique body of data furnishing the globe-trotting executive or academic cultural specialist with easy-to-access, compact guides to thinking patterns of all the world's major cultures. The NCP database is a valuable online resource for:

- Globalising corporations
- Training Officers
- Executives who negotiate internationally
- People who have to give presentations in different countries
- International business departments in universities and colleges
- Management consultants
- Personal development of the individual
- Those who host foreign visitors or assignees
- Expatriate trainers
- Those involved in mergers and acquisitions
- Executives who need to diagnose reaction or behaviour of foreign partners
- Top level managers and strategists
- People working on international committees or in intergovernmental organisations

Online Cultural Assessment

Do you know your personal cultural profile? Which are your dominant characteristics? How do your cultural traits compare with the norms for your own nationality? More importantly, if you are in international business, how do they compare with French, German, Spanish, Chinese, Japanese or Arab traits?

It takes about an hour for you to have the answers to these questions by taking our Personal Cultural Assessment. With this valuable orientation you will be well placed to assess the impression you will make on a selection of other nationals and the impact they will make on you.

Email: info@cultureactive.com
Web: www.cultureactive.com

When Cultures Collide

In *When Cultures Collide*, Richard Lewis provides a truly global and practical guide to working and communicating across cultures, explaining how our own culture and language affect the ways in which we organise our world, think, feel and respond, before going on to suggest both general and specific ways of making our influence felt across the cultural divide.

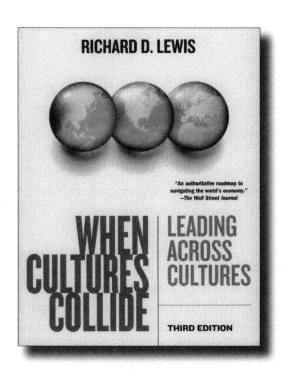

There are penetrating insights into how different business cultures accord status, structure their organisations and view the role of the leader, alongside invaluable advice on global negotiation, sales and marketing. The book ranges from differences in etiquette and body language to new thinking in the area of international management and team-building in Europe and the USA, as well as covering challenging new geographical ground in Russia, China and the Far East.

By focusing on the cultural roots of national behaviour, both in society and business, we can foresee and calculate with a surprising degree of accuracy how others will react and respond to us. Lewis adds the often overlooked dimension of language – for example, how Japanese often react in a certain way because they are thinking in Japanese.

When Cultures Collide gives you a greater understanding of what makes other people tick and enables managers to ensure that their policies and activities exploit cultural synergies and make the right appeal to their chosen market.

Publisher: Nicholas Brealey International
Paperback: 600 pages (third edition)
ISBN-13:   978-1-904838-02-9
ISBN-10:   1-904838-02-2

The Cultural Imperative
Global Trends in the 21ˢᵗ Century

Will the tidal waves of globalisation
lead us to a bland and uniform cultural
landscape dominated by a unified cultural
perspective? Will cultural imperialism
triumph in the 21ˢᵗ century? Or will the
cultural imperative that drives human
behaviour through religion, language,
geography and history maintain its
influence on the human consciousness?

In *The Cultural Imperative*, Richard Lewis
explores these questions and proposes
his own thesis in this sweeping book
that examines the forces that keep us
from taking off our "cultural spectacles"
and explains how cultural traits are
so deeply embedded as to resist the
homogenisation predicted by so many
others.

He also looks at culture's effect on
cognitive processes, the rise of the Pacific
Rim as the 21ˢᵗ century cultural ecology,
Americanisation v. Asianisation, possible
future cultural alliances and more.

As with his other books, Lewis uses easy-to-understand diagrams throughout
to illustrate his concepts and ideas. His original three-category classification
of cultures – linear-active, multi-active and reactive – comes to life through his
elegant design.

Publisher: Intercultural Press
Paperback: 338 pages
ISBN-13:   978-1-931930-35-2
ISBN-10:   1-931930-35-X

Humour across Frontiers

Round the World in 80 Jokes

"Wildly funny and unexpected. A delight to read. The distinction of the book comes from the way it pinpoints national differences through hilarious humour."

Michael Gearin-Tosh, Professor in the Overseas Department of Stanford University

"Richard Lewis has spent a lifetime teaching international businessmen how to translate such diverse languages as Finnish into Vietnamese, and Portuguese into Australian; now he achieves something even more difficult – explaining how and how not to share the often impenetrable humour that sets different peoples' funny bones tingling. Enjoy it, as I did, on your next long airplane ride. The sub-title is Around The World in 80 Jokes but in fact there are more than 800."

Sir Eldon Griffiths, former Chairman, now Patron, World Affairs Councils of America

"Some people have humour, some do not. Richard Lewis is gifted with plenty of this precious quality. As if this would not be enough, he has collected the best jokes from all around the world and, as the foremost expert on cross-culture, he has compiled the material into a book which will attract an international audience. Read and smile!"

Uno Grönkvist, former Senior Vice President Corporate Relations, Swedish Telekom

"Humour across Frontiers is the perfect companion to Richard Lewis's earlier encyclopaedic analysis of cultural characteristics across the globe, When Cultures Collide, and should be in the luggage on any trip. Both books will be in mine."

Roger Ainsworth, Master, St. Catherine's College, Oxford University

"In business, I often work with international teams and I have noticed that shared humour is a great clue to common understanding among people. So it leads to better teamwork. Nevertheless, humour is very dependent on culture…and Richard Lewis taught us that cultures sometimes collide! So does humour. At a time of business activities without borders, it is necessary to understand humour across frontiers. It is the best way to build trust and intimacy between people. So let's go round the world in 80 jokes…and hopefully with 80 smiles!"

Michel Caron, Corporate Vice President, Michelin

"With this text the world seems to become a better place to live in. Humour across Frontiers offers us a witty and pleasant journey throughout countries and mentalities – an undoubted contribution for a better intercultural understanding."

Carlos Baleia, Portuguese playwright

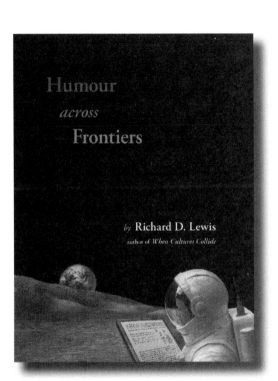

"This is a wonderful book. We live in an age in which we are so defensive of our identity and so protective of our differences that we are in danger of losing a sense of common humanity. This book shows that we do share many things, not least a sense of humour. While the book is very sensitive to differences between cultures, it is overall a terrific celebration of what we as human beings have in common."

Lord Plant of Highfield

"Richard Lewis offers the reader a parade of international, but culture-bound jokes. Open the book, don't rush and you have embarked on a most enjoyable intercultural journey."

Jukka Valtasaari, Finnish Ambassador to the USA

"Great leaders have learned to use humour effectively. This book is a must for global business leaders!"

Bob Beck, Chief People Officer, BearingPoint

Publisher: Transscreen Publications
Paperback: 242 pages
ISBN-13:   978-0-9534398-2-9
ISBN-10:   0-9534398-2-8